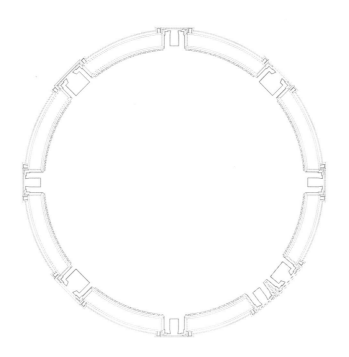

BUDDHIST STUPAS IN ASIA: THE SHAPE OF PERFECTION
1st edition – October 2001

Published by
Lonely Planet Publications Pty Ltd ABN 36 005 607 983
90 Maribyrnong St, Footscray, Vic 3011, Australia

Lonely Planet Offices
Australia: Locked Bag 1, Footscray, Victoria 3011
USA: 150 Linden Street, Oakland, CA 94607
UK: 10a Spring Place, London NW5 3BH
France: 1 rue du Dahomey, 75011, Paris

Printed by The Bookmaker International Ltd
Printed in Thailand

Photographs
Many of the photographs in this book are available for licensing from
Lonely Planet Images.
email: lpi@lonelyplanet.com.au

ISBN 1 86450 120 0

Designer: Daniel New
Editor: Bridget Blair
Senior Editor: Martine Lleonart
Design Advisers: David Kemp & Andrew Weatherill
Editorial Advisers: Bruce Evans & Martin Heng
Illustrators: Kieran Grogan, Yvonne Bischofberger & Brett Moore
Photographic Adviser: Richard I'Anson

BUDDHIST STUPAS IN ASIA THE SHAPE OF PERFECTION

Photography **Bill Wassman**

Text **Joe Cummings**

Foreword **Robert AF Thurman**

LONELY PLANET PUBLICATIONS • MELBOURNE • OAKLAND • LONDON • PARIS

CONTENTS

FOREWORD

Stupas are memorials of enlightenment achieved, and also bring enlightenment to life in the present. The word for 'memory' is the same as the word for 'mindfulness' (Sanskrit *smrti*, Pali *sati*, Tibetan *dran pa*). Mindfulness is the intensified awareness that sparks the Buddhist process of educating oneself to overcome the world of ignorance which causes suffering. In the Buddha's view, all suffering that afflicts beings is caused by ignorance or 'misknowledge' – a wrong knowing of the nature of reality that systematically distorts experience and actions. Liberation from such suffering requires overcoming misknowledge by means of correct awareness and accurate knowledge; that is, wisdom. The good news of Buddhism is that true reality is itself freedom from suffering, that the world of suffering is less real than the world of bliss, that liberation is not something artificial that requires an elaborate, perhaps unrealistic, construction, but is natural, is already there, needs only to be understood to be realised. Truth is bliss, suffering is falsehood. Truth prevails.

When the Buddha knew he was dying, he gave instructions about the disposition of his body, which was apparently a great marvel. Most of his followers avoided creating any naturalistic image of it for many centuries (instead signalling his presence in a scene by a footprint, a wheel, a lotus, a tree) perhaps because, as accounts indicate, his body tended to metamorphose in order to appear to each person in the most inspiring way possible. As the end of his life approached, he said that his body should be cremated, and the relics divided up and enclosed in four great monuments, such as those stupa-mounds – man-made axial mountains – which are constructed to memorialise a great monarch. These monuments were to be erected at crossroad centres at Lumbini, where he was born; Bodhgaya, where he attained enlightenment under the bodhi tree; Sarnath, where he gave his first teaching ('turning of the wheel of dharma'); and Kushinagar, where he attained *parinirvana*, or freedom from involuntary embodiment. Such monuments are meant to symbolise the axial mountain of ancient cos-mologies, the core of the world that connects earth and heaven. It is said that eight different kings with armies showed up at the cremation, so the relics had to be divided up eight ways to avoid a war!

The Buddha's task was to educate beings to overcome their 'beginningless ignorance', to awaken them to their natural state of freedom from suffering. Everything he did and said was to increase awareness and wisdom, as that caused beings' release into bliss. Apparently, he was rather good at what he was doing, since many beings did attain release during his teaching time among them. After he passed into nirvana from the physical form of Prince Siddhartha to become Shakyamuni Buddha, his liberative movement began to spread throughout the world, a spread that has had its ups and downs but still continues today.

The stupa monument (Tibetan *mchod rten* or *chorten*, a base for worship) has proliferated everywhere the movement has flourished. Its square, round, triangular, crescent and drop shapes symbolise the 'great elements' of earth, water, fire, air, space and sometimes consciousness. They are arranged in the stupa in various ways, but are always intended to demonstrate the triumph of enlightenment's wisdom over suffering's ignorance. They transform the landscapes of the world from the theatre of suffering (which most cultures settle for as inevitable) to a realm for awakening from ignorance and escaping from suffering into the more real world of bliss. People in all the different cultures that have discovered Buddhism seem to have gone crazy with joy, building stupas by the millions. Though many do contain relics of some enlightened being, they have gone beyond being mere funeral reliquaries. They are memorials, rather, to the immanent possibility of freedom from suffering for all beings. They signal the triumphal reality of a nature that enables beings to evolve to experience the ultimate fulfilment of perfect bliss, beyond death and unsatisfying life. A landscape full of stupas becomes more peaceful, the people more gentle. Stupas stand as eloquent testimony to the higher purpose of life, beyond competing and struggling, getting and spending. Consciously or subliminally, they help turn people's minds away from their frustrating obsessions and towards their own higher potential.

There is an amusing story told about an old man who had led a rather unhelpful life; disliked by everyone and marked by the ugliness of constant conflicts, he nevertheless wanted to become a monk for good luck, hedging his bets as he neared the end of his days. The head monks were having difficulty ordaining him, since the tradition was that they had to discover something good in any candidate for the monkhood. Mobilising all their clairvoyant powers, which made them capable of knowing others' former lives, they could find no good deed, even going back many, many lifetimes. Still wanting to turn the man around, they took him to see the Buddha before giving up. The Buddha looked at the man and into his evolutionary past, his own clairvoyance far more powerful than even his most saintly followers, and after some time said, 'Ah! It's all right. You can ordain him – I've found something good in his past.' 'What was it?' they inquired. The Buddha replied, 'Long ago, he was reborn as an ant, and he came with his clan to the site of the great stupa of Bodhnath (in present day Nepal), where some people had gathered to picnic and pay homage to the stupa. At the moment when the head of the family got up from his meal to begin his pious circumambulations, our man here was crawling across his boot, trying to get more crumbs. He was able to hang on to the boot while the pilgrim made it three times around the stupa! This was good deed enough for him!'

At the other end of the spectrum of stupa stories, there is the famous Zen story, from Tang dynasty China. When the National Master Hui Chung was nearing his end, his disciple Emperor Su Tsung asked him, 'After you die, what will you need?' After a moment of silence, the Master said, 'Build me a seamless monument!' Baffled, the Emperor asked, 'Could you tell me what such a monument would look like?' 'My disciple will tell you later' was the answer. Years later, after the Master had gone, the Emperor asked the new master, Tan Yuan, who said, 'South of Hsiang, north of T'an, in between there's gold sufficient to build a nation. Beneath the shadowless tree, the community ferryboat. Within the crystal palace, there's no-one who knows.'

Here the Master asks the ruler not to be dualistic about the world of perfection of enlightenment and bliss and the ordinary world of suffering. Hsiang T'an is the birth-place of the Master, where one might expect an ordinary monument to be built in commemoration. 'South and north' of the same place means 'everywhere'. 'Gold sufficient' means 'don't fail to bring your entire empire into the realm of freedom because you think you can't afford it'. The 'shadowless tree' is the enlightenment that understands the reality of nature to be everywhere freedom from suffering. 'The community ferryboat' means that the Emperor should maintain the institution that brings people across from the world of suffering into the world of awakening. 'No-one knows within the crystal palace' means that you can't wait for a moment of egocentric knowing apart from the final reality of perfect bliss, you have to proceed with wisdom's compassionate participation, knowing by being, awakened to the infinite relationality of freedom.

This beautiful book takes us around some of the millions of stupas that transform our planet, whether we are like ants carried on the boots of the author pilgrims or can seamlessly appreciate the landscape with Bodhisattva dedication to all beings' liberation. It is a pleasure and a privilege to wander through its pages from place to place, experiencing the faith and determination of so many individuals in so many civilisations who have shown their aspiration and vision by creatively and patiently placing one stone upon another in the myriad shapes of perfection.

Robert AF Thurman
Ganden Dekyi Ling,
Catskill Mountains, New York
March, 2001

Robert Thurman is the president of Tibet House in New York and Jey Tsong Khapa Professor of Indo-Tibetan Buddhist Studies at Columbia University.

All the topes in the entire world are of one lustre and all of them lead to heaven and emancipation;
the people who are mindful of their duties should in all respects and at all times pay homage.

Thupavamsa (Stupa Chronicle)

INTRODUCTION

A roughly conical pile of fire-reddened, dictionary-sized bricks, edges softened by time, stands in a green meadow on a slight rise overlooking a river. Bits of yellowed plaster, moulded into flower garlands, cling to where a brick line holds its shape, or lie amid broken chunks around the base of the pile. Almost buried beneath drifting soil, tall grass and tangled fig roots, a few stone blocks reflect sunlight from neat ridges scraped into the surface.

One stone rectangle, larger than the others, has been tipped sideways. On its nearly level, rippling surface lies a cluster of fresh yellow and cream plumeria blossoms. You can detect their sweetness on the breeze, mixed with the perfume from a trio of burning incense sticks jutting from a ceramic bowl filled with sand. Whoever left the offering is nowhere to be seen, but in the stillness one can almost sense the devotion arcing across two millennia, from the unseen artisan whose iron tools cut the stone to a visitor who retreated not more than 10 minutes ago.

'Sermons in stone, brick and mortar', one Buddhist scholar has called them. Diagrams of synchronicity in which 'time is fixed, crystallised, rendered static', claims a Western architect. Attempts to encapsulate the durable appeal of the stupa are confounded by the vast and varied history of stupa-building and stupa-worshipping, all but silencing the would-be inquisitor. Yet the stupa continues to inspire us to take photographs, sketch diagrams and write thousands of words, digging to uncover a key that might unlock its mysteries.

Once you're on the stupa trail you can't stop. At first you're in awe of the size, the history, the simplicity of the whole and the complexity of the detail. After you've stood before 10, or 20 or 50, you begin to notice the differences as well as the similarities. It seems unbelievable that a lone *chandi* in central Java could look so much like a stupa in southern India, that you can see a Bagan *zedi* reflected in a *prasada* at Angkor Wat. You develop preferences and then, in a few years, abandon them. Gradually the solid, silent masses begin speaking to you, and eventually you may find yourself talking back to them. The dialogue can last a lifetime.

Undoubtedly one basic if unspoken reason many of us become stupa-watchers is the fact that the monuments are simply so accessible. For most sightings, it isn't necessary to breach hallowed halls, walk musty corridors, ask for a key to the gate, hop a wall, bribe a guard or obtain a permit. Stupas aren't closed on Sundays, or Saturdays or full moon days; in fact they're more dependable than the neighbourhood 7-Eleven. You don't have to be Buddhist to approach one, and in even the strictest religious settings they're open to all, regardless of race, nationality, gender or social class.

Some stupas require more effort to reach than others. For a glimpse of Kyaiktiyo Paya in Myanmar, best seen at dawn, you'll have to climb a mountain at least part way (or hire a sedan chair if you don't mind sharing the religious merit – and a fistful of *kyat* – with local carriers). Some of the Tibetan stupas pictured in this book lie several days' journey from the Tibetan capital of Lhasa, and getting to Lhasa itself requires some paperwork and not an inconsiderable sum of money. Another hilltop stupa, That Meuang Sing in northern Laos, stands near the end of a rough road that crosses several unbridged streams. To experience some of Nepal's more atmospheric stupa sites will require several days of hiking. Afghanistan's civil war has meant that some of Buddhism's earliest archaeological sites have remained off limits for some time.

Access to many other impressive topes, however, has never been easier. Guided tours are available to many of Asia's great stupas. In Japan the *gorinto* can be found in the most urban of landscapes, and every Thai stupa pictured in this volume can be reached within a day's travel of one of Thailand's provincial capitals. Hotel accommodation can be found less than 15 minutes' walk from Java's world treasure, Borobudur, and electric lifts carry visitors to Myanmar's indescribable Shwedagon Paya.

An encounter with a stupa is an encounter with myth – or as Carl Jung and Joseph Campbell might have phrased it, an archetypal truth. What may at first seem only to be an artistic and perhaps nostalgic arrangement of brick, stone or wood may eventually come to be seen as an elaborate vessel, transporting the *buddhadharma* across three millennia.

FROM PALACE TO FOREST:
THE STORY OF THE BUDDHA

According to Pali chronicles, the historical figure known as Gautama Buddha was born in 623 BC in Lumbini, near the present-day India-Nepal border, into a family of noble standing. His father, King Suddhodana, ruled a regional clan known as the Shakyas.

Brahmin soothsayers told his queen, Maya Devi, shortly before she bore her only son that the baby would grow up to be either a very great ruler or an enlightened being. When the infant was born, King Suddhodana named him Siddhartha, 'Perfect Wealth', in expectation that the boy would some day inherit his crown. He showered Prince Siddhartha with worldly gifts to ensure that he would experience all the pleasures of royal status. Fearing that the prince might forsake the regal path laid out before him, the king did his utmost to ensure that Siddhartha never left Kapilavastu, the opulent and fortified palace complex in which the family lived. In this way he hoped to prevent his son from seeing the poverty and human suffering that lay beyond the palace gates.

At the age of 16, Prince Siddhartha married a beautiful princess named Yasodhara, whose hand he won after successfully completing a series of difficult athletic contests. However, Siddhartha was an inquisitive young man and, as the legend goes, he made four independent forays outside the palace walls when he was 29 years old. On the first, he encountered a very old man, the first person of advanced age he'd ever seen. His second venture into the world brought him face to face with a diseased person, and on the third he became very disturbed upon seeing a corpse, as his father had never told him about death. When questioned by his master, Siddhartha's chariot driver confirmed that all humanity was subject to old age, sickness and death. On his fourth trip outside the palace the young prince came upon a wandering ascetic who had given up the trappings of worldly life to search for truth. Siddhartha immediately made up his mind to follow the renunciate's example.

The next evening Siddhartha left behind his sleeping wife and newly born son, mounted his horse Kanthaka and headed for the city gates. Although his father had ordered the gates sealed, they miraculously opened before the prince, and angelic beings lifted Kanthaka by the hooves so no-one would hear Siddhartha leaving Kapilavastu.

After riding all night, Siddhartha dismounted, traded his fine robe for the tunic of a hunter he met in the forest and, in a final act of renunciation, chopped off his hair with a dagger. He then wandered northern India for six years, studying Brahmanic meditation with Hindu gurus and subjecting himself to many austerities and acts of self-mortification, including long fasts.

Frustrated that these practices had brought him no closer to the existential truths he craved to know, he seated himself at the base of a ficus tree and vowed not to budge from the spot until such truths were revealed to him. During his deep meditation, many bizarre visions came, including the appearance of Mara, the Buddhist equivalent of Satan. Mara tried frightening Siddhartha out of his meditation and when that didn't work, he summoned his lascivious daughters who attempted to seduce the prince-turned-ascetic away from his quest.

Ignoring these visions, Siddhartha focused his attention on the nature of mind and body in the present moment. Seeing that even the most blissful and refined states of mind were subject to decay, he abandoned all desire for what he now saw as unreliable and unsatisfying. Via this simple act, the meditating Siddhartha experienced *bodhichitra* (awakened mind), a profound spiritual rebirth.

His long and difficult endeavour having reached fruition, the Buddha (or 'Awakened One') wandered onward to Sarnath, near Varanasi, where a group of five ascetics with whom he had previously studied recognised his new-found enlightenment and asked for his teachings. He responded with what is considered the Buddha's first sermon, thus setting in motion the basic dharma, or Buddhist philosophy.

At Sarnath the Buddha spoke of four noble truths that had the power to liberate any human being who could realise them.

All life is subject to suffering (*dukkha*)

Suffering is caused by selfish desire (*tanha*, 'grasping' or 'craving')

Abandon grasping and suffering will cease to arise

The way to eliminate grasping is to follow the Eightfold Path

He furthermore taught that the Noble Eightfold Path consisted of:

Right understanding

Right mindedness (right thought)

Right speech

Right bodily conduct

Right livelihood

Right effort

Right attentiveness

Right concentration

The Buddha continued to wander around northern India, imparting his teachings freely to all who crossed his path, including philosophers and kings of the day.
A community of those who followed his teaching, later referred to as 'the Sangha', formed around him and in centres where he taught, often associated with pre-Buddhist *chaityas*.
When he reached 80 years of age, according to the chronicles, he fell mortally ill in Kushinagar, only around 100km from where he was born.

On his deathbed the Buddha admonished his followers to 'strive on with diligence', before passing away into *parinirvana*, the complete nirvana beyond death.

BIRTH OF THE STUPA: INDIA

BIRTH OF THE STUPA: INDIA

Immediately following the death and cremation of the Buddha c. 543 BC, according to most Buddhist chronicles, King Ajatasattu of Magadha and a Brahmin priest named Drona took custody of the Buddha's remains. They reportedly divided the relics into eight portions and assigned eight kings the responsibility for building stupas to enshrine the sacred objects in eight different locations in what are today northern India and southern Nepal. If these eight great stupas were in fact erected, absolutely no visible trace of them has yet been discovered.

The verifiable, visible history of the Buddhist stupa commences roughly three centuries later during the reign of King Ashoka (c. 269–232 BC), the third and greatest monarch of northern India's Maurya dynasty. Asia's first known Buddhist king, or *dharmaraja*, initiated public works throughout his dominions, including as far north-west as present-day Pakistan. Among these works he propagated Buddhism by constructing stupas, monasteries and other Buddhist monuments. Legend has it that Ashoka had the eight original reliquaries unsealed so that he could subdivide the contents and inter the relics in 84,000 stupas (to honour the 84,000 constituents of dharma) throughout South and South-East Asia.

Notwithstanding the fact that it is difficult to believe – and today impossible to confirm – that Ashoka sponsored the construction of so many stupas, India's most famous king appears to have been responsible for the oldest Buddhist architectural remains found anywhere in Asia. His first structures were not stupas but solitary, Persian-style *stambas*, or pillars, polished, grooved and surmounted by animal sculptures thought to have been crafted by Greco-Syrian stone-carvers. Dating to around 250 BC, the most well known of the 'Ashokan pillars' stands at Sarnath in north-eastern India, about 10km from Varanasi, at the site where the Buddha gave the *prathama deshana*, or first teachings. Once reaching over 20m, the pillar's toppled capital – currently on display in the Sarnath Archaeological Museum – features four back-to-back lions, today the national emblem of India. The lions stand on an abacus decorated with smaller relief sculptures of a lion, elephant, horse and bull alternating with *dharmachakra* (wheel-shaped symbols representing Buddhist doctrine). The four animals may stand for the four cardinal directions – emphasising the spread of Buddhism to 'the four quarters' of the world – or for the four rivers flowing from mythical Mt Meru.

Epigraphs on this and other columns erected by King Ashoka admonish the Buddhist community not to succumb to schism, assuring the king's enduring reputation as Buddhism's great unifier. In his determination to spread the Buddhist gospel, Ashoka is believed to have sponsored a legion of *dharmaduta* or 'dharma ambassadors', learned monks who travelled to every corner of his empire and possibly beyond to pass on the teachings. Ashoka's own son and daughter are believed to have been sent to Sri Lanka to convert the Sinhalese royal family to Buddhism.

In addition to the half-dozen edict pillars still standing in India, the Ashokan reign bequeathed numerous other lasting works of Buddhist art and architecture, among them some of India's most famous stupa sites.

Sanchi, in central India about 45km from Bhopal, ranks eminent. Here the Great Stupa (*mahachaitya*), constructed in the middle of the 3rd century BC, served as the basic model for stupa design for around 700 years. On a base measuring 36.5m in diameter, the stupa rises to 16.4m. A vast and near-perfect *anda* ('egg' or dome), constructed of stone blocks, is surrounded by a circular stone balustrade, or *vedika*, used to guide worshipers in their ritual and contemplative circumambulation of the stupa. Four large, tiered stone gateways known as *torana* admit the faithful through the balustrade to the base of the dome. Stairways lead to a second level, also encircled by a *vedika*. Although the dome itself is quite plain, the gateways and balustrade are richly carved with scenes from Buddhist mythology.

SANCHI, THE ASHOKAN EXEMPLAR

None of these reliefs contain any image of the Buddha himself. Instead, other icons in the masterfully carved scenes make his presence known. On the architrave of the eastern gate, for example, Siddhartha's departure from his father's palace shows only the prince's horse and a parasol held over the saddle by a royal servant; the parasol (an Indian symbol of royal status) serves to indicate the teacher's proximity. In other reliefs, the lotus stands for his birth, the Bodhi tree for his awakening, the dharma wheel for his first sermon and the stupa for his death. Iconic representations of the Buddha in human-like form didn't occur in Buddhist art until several centuries later.

ABOVE *Sanchi is decorated with images of stupas receiving supplication from Brahmanic deities.*

RIGHT *Although smaller in size, Stupa No 3 at Sanchi follows much the same form as the Great Stupa save for the* chattravali *(umbrella), which features only one tier.*

FAR RIGHT *The exquisitely carved* torana *at Sanchi portray scenes from the* jatakas, *or Buddha life stories.*

OPPOSITE *In this view of the Great Stupa at Sanchi, the* torana *(gate),* harmika *(square enclosure atop the dome) and multitiered* chattravali *(umbrella) are all clearly visible.*

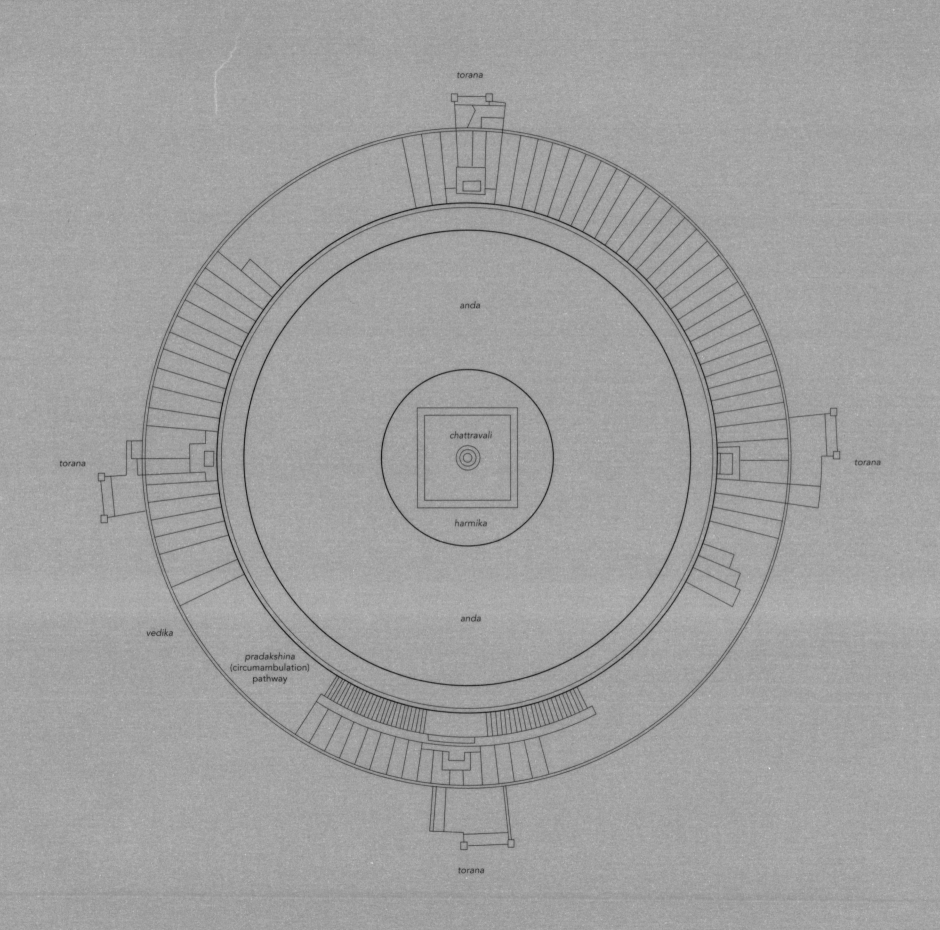

torana

anda

torana

chattravali

torana

harmika

anda

vedika

pradakshina
(circumambulation)
pathway

torana

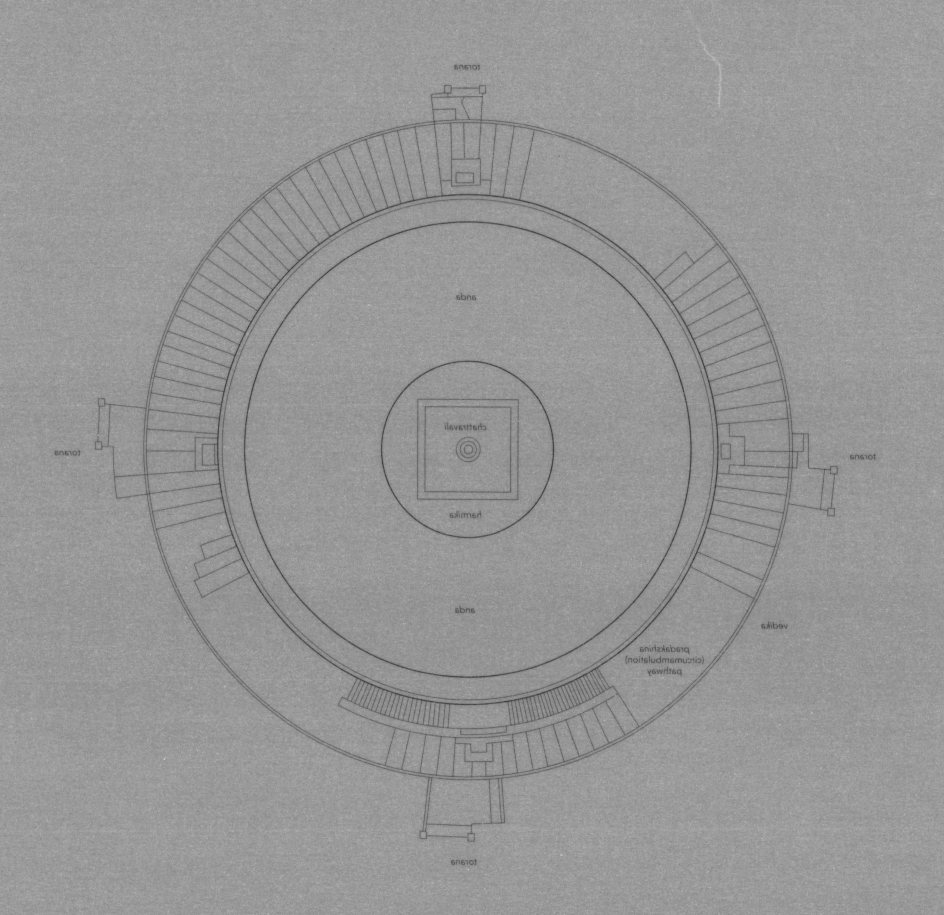

torana

anda

torana

chattravali

harmika

torana

anda

vedika

pradakshina
(circumambulation)
pathway

torana

RIGHT *A relief of a stupa receiving supplication at Sanchi.*

BELOW (TOP) *A host of guardian deities protects the entrance to the Great Stupa's promenade.*

BELOW (MIDDLE) *The middle architrave of the Great Stupa's auspicious eastern* torana *portrays Siddhartha's departure from his family's palace on his quest for enlightenment. A riderless horse represents the prince.*

BOTTOM *On this arched lintel elephants pay homage to a Sanchi stupa.*

OPPOSITE *Looking down at the* torana *from the railed walkway around the Great Stupa.*

Centred atop the dome, a square, fence-like *harmika*, also fashioned from stone, encloses a carved stone *chattravali* (umbrella), with three canopies, receding in size from bottom to top. Two smaller stupas at Sanchi follow a similar model, except one displays a single-canopy *chattravali* while the other is missing its original superstructure altogether. Empty cylindrical holes through the centre of each monument once contained wooden pillars, long since lost to insects or rot. Beneath its pillar axis, the Great Stupa was thought to have contained Buddha relics, but when excavated – well after the Muslim invasion of northern India – it was found empty. The two smaller stupas at Sanchi contained the relics of Buddhist monks who may have been contemporaries of the Buddha or who may have been locally respected teachers from the Ashokan era.

Some historians theorise that Ashoka built the Great Stupa over an existing earthen mound, possibly one half its size, erected a century or more before the Ashokan era. An inscription at Ashoka's Nigali Sagar pillar mentions the 'doubling' of an existing stupa at Kanakamuni, so it is possible this was a practice the king initiated. If so, he may have been the first in a long line of stupa sponsors who built new stupas to encase older, possibly ruined or abandoned stupas. All three stupas at Sanchi have been rebuilt several times since their establishment during the Maurya dynasty. An inscription at Amaravati, for example, mentions a reconstruction of the *vedika* at Sanchi in the 2nd or 3rd century AD.

After Sanchi in central India, Gandhara became the next arena for the development of the stupa and other Buddhist art forms. This region is located around what is now Peshawar in Pakistan. It was ruled by Greek princes from Bactria (present-day Balkh in northern Afghanistan), itself the easternmost province of the Greek empire, during the 3rd century BC when Ashoka's Buddhist missionaries arrived. The semi-autonomous state converted to Buddhism and over the next 200 years fused Buddhist thought and Greek art to produce unique works of sculpture and architecture.

GANDHARA & BEYOND

ABOVE *Part of a larger Buddhist monastery, the Butkara (Butkada) Stupa in Pakistan's Swat Valley was originally erected by local Buddhists in the 2nd century BC. The stupa was encased in five successive, larger stupas before Muslim persecution, vandalism and eventual abandonment reduced the site to a pile of bricks.*

ABOVE RIGHT *Carved into a large niche at Taxila's Mohra Moradu complex, erected during the 1st and 2nd centuries BC, this inverted-goblet-shaped stupa is reminiscent of western India's cave stupas.*

RIGHT *Round-topped, straight-sided Shingerdar Stupa in Swat was built by King Uttarasena in the 2nd century AD to house Buddha relics.*

OPPOSITE *Although difficult to discern in its ruined state, the Dharmarajika Stupa at Taxila probably featured a hemispherical dome in the classic Ashokan style. Adjacent pediments supported monastery buildings.*

If Ashoka's architects designed and constructed any monuments in the area, nothing remains save a fragment from a typically Ashokan *stamba*. Inscriptions indicate that the most visible stupa ruins, at Taxila, were erected during the 1st and 2nd centuries BC, well after Ashoka's reign came to an end. Unlike the perfect hemispheres of Sanchi, the Taxila stupa domes tend more towards the cylindrical, and sit upon massive square pediments fitted with large, door-like niches. There is no evidence of any *vedikas*; instead relief sculptures depicting scenes from the life of Gautama Buddha were applied directly to the pediments of these stupas.

RIGHT *Dhamekh Stupa, at Sarnath, near Varanasi, commemorates the site where the Buddha supposedly delivered his first discourse on dharma, or Buddhist philosophy. Although excavations have revealed brickwork dating to around 200 BC, most of the monument dates to around AD 500. Even in its semi-ruined state, the surviving sandstone-block stupa reaches 34m.*

BELOW *Cave No 4 at Ajanta displays the typical layout of the early Buddhist cave temples of India.*

BOTTOM *The ruins of the Sphola Stupa, known during the British Raj as the 'Khyber Top', stand sentry at the entrance to the Khyber Pass on the Pakistan-Afghanistan border. Dating from the 2nd to 5th centuries AD, the stupa was erected as part of a large Buddhist monastery complex under the reign of King Kanishka and is one of the Indian subcontinent's largest stupas. This hand-coloured wood engraving is from* Nouvelle Geographie Universelle: La Terre et Les Hommes *by Elisée Reclus, published by Hachette, 1883.*

OPPOSITE *When the Buddha reached 80 years of age, he died and entered parinirvana at Kushinagar in northern India. His last words were 'Decay is inherent in all things. Work out your own salvation with diligence.' After cremating the great teacher, the Buddha's followers are said to have enshrined his ashes in the Mukutbandhan Chaitya, today more commonly known as Ramabhar Stupa. Kushinagar grew to become an important Buddhist monastic centre and is today the site of Thai, Burmese and Sri Lankan monasteries. All that remains of the stupa is a ruined dome, with a base measuring 47m in diameter. The visible portion of this stupa is most likely an encasement of a much earlier stupa, though none of the remains have been properly dated.*

In the relief panels chronicling the Buddha's life, we see images of the teacher himself – standing, sitting and reclining – for the first time in the developing history of Buddhist art. Showing strong Greek influence, this school of sculpture extended roughly from 50 BC to AD 500 and is known as 'Greco-Buddhist' or 'Gandharan'. Today the best places to view collections of Gandharan sculpture are the Indian Museum in Calcutta, the British Museum in London and the Louvre in Paris.

Excavations undertaken between 1913 and 1934 uncovered over 30 Buddhist monasteries in and around Taxila, many of which are thought to have been associated with a *mahachaitya*, or great stupa. The largest, the brick-domed Dharmarajika Stupa, measures 35m in diameter and is surrounded by the ruins of smaller stupas. Dharmarajika may have been constructed or reconstructed in the 1st century AD over an earlier hemispherical stupa, possibly of Ashokan design. When it was rebuilt, Dharmarajika's horizontal design changed from a solid core on a square base to a wheel-shaped foundation similar to those found at stupa sites in Mathura, Amaravati and Nagarjunakonda farther south.

Gandharan stupa design appears to have spread as far as the outskirts of present-day Kabul, Afghanistan, where the Guldara Stupa features a tall square base with portals on each side. Although the dome and superstructure for this stupa have been completely destroyed, the foundation design appears to be similar to stupas at Taxila.

The great Ashokan stupas of Sanchi and their equivalents in Pakistan and Afghanistan inspired the basic design elements that have comprised most stupas from ancient to modern times. Throughout Buddhism's early centuries stupa domes were topped with a smaller cube-like *harmika*. Surmounting the *harmika* was a stylised umbrella or *chattravali*. In some early stupas the umbrella canopy is transformed into tree foliage, and its shaft becomes a tree trunk, just as Gautama Buddha exchanged his royal parasol for the protection of the Bodhi tree.

CARRYING ON THE CODE

ABOVE *The oldest* griha-stupas *(cave stupas) in India, at Bhaja near Mumbai, date to the 2nd century BC. Note the* chattravali *carved into the cave ceiling over the individual stupas.*

FAR RIGHT *These stone reliefs of Gautama Buddha at the Ajanta cave temples reflect the refined Gupta school of art popular in Buddhist India from the 3rd to 6th centuries AD.*

RIGHT *Constructed between the 2nd and 7th centuries AD, the Ajanta cave temples of north-eastern India contain some of India's most impressive Buddhist art. This stupa and its cell, carved from solid rock, show a fully developed multitiered base, dome,* harmika *and triple* chattravali. *A relief of a sitting Gautama Buddha and surrounding pavilion unites base and dome.*

OPPOSITE *This cave stupa at Ellora is thought to have been carved from solid rock around AD 700. As at Ajanta, the walls of the cathedral-like chamber have been carved to resemble wood bracing.*

All of these elements can be seen at India's remaining great stupa sites, including the imposing *mahachaitya* of Dhamekh (AD 200–500), near Sarnath, and the rock-carved, goblet-shaped stupas found in well-preserved Buddhist cave temples (50 BC–AD 700) at Karli, Bedsa, Bhaja, Nasik, Ajanta and Ellora. Huge stupa bases, left behind by Hindu kings who disassembled the superstructures for bricks to build their palaces, can also be seen at Amaravati and Nagarjunakonda (both 2nd century AD).

As the stupa travelled great distances over the centuries, its surface complexities multiplied. The dome evolved from India's pure hemispheres to a near cylinder in the early Pyu stupas of central Myanmar, to the blunt-topped *prang* of Cambodia, the concave-sided bell shape of northern Myanmar and Thailand, and finally to the inverted alms bowl shape common among Himalayan stupas. More idiosyncratic developments, such as the intricate, cube-like stupas of Bagan, the raised mandala of Borobudur and the vertical towers of east Asia, occurred along the way. No matter how far away from India the stupa strays, however, its basic Indian antecedents can always be recognised.

ABOVE *Stone relief at Mahabodhi of an angelic being surrounded by lotus petals.*

ABOVE RIGHT *Draped in a Tibetan prayer scarf and flanked by stupa reliefs, a gilded Buddha in* bhumisparsa *(touching the earth) pose sits in one of the adjacent shrines at Mahabodhi, Bodhgaya.*

RIGHT *It's generally believed that a stupa was first built here at Bodhgaya between the 5th and 7th centuries AD, although King Ashoka may have ordered the construction of a simpler dome stupa in the 3rd century BC. Bengali Buddhist kings of the Pala dynasty are thought to have carried out a restoration between the 8th and 12th centuries. Invading Muslim armies destroyed the stupa in the 13th century. It lay in ruins until the late 19th century, when the British Raj sponsored a reconstruction using Burmese advisers.*

OPPOSITE *Multicoloured prayer flags adorn the spot at Mahabodhi where the Buddha reportedly attained enlightenment.*

SRI LANKA

SRI LANKA

In King Ashoka's drive to spread the Buddhist gospel beyond his northern Indian empire, the monarch employed his own family members as travelling *dharmaduta* or 'dharma ambassadors'. Wherever Buddhism flowed stupas soon followed, and in Sri Lanka both doctrine and art found perhaps their most fertile ground for further propagation in southern Asia.

Arriving on the lush island of Lanka around 250 BC, Ashoka's son Mahinda and four other monks are said to have met with Lanka's King Devanampiya Tissa and his courtiers on a rocky crag at Mihinthale. Initially piquing the Lankan king's interest with a riddle about mango trees, Mahinda eventually convinced the king to abandon his Hindu beliefs in favour of Buddhism.

After Devanampiya Tissa's kingdom, which was centred at Anuradhapura in north-central Sri Lanka, accepted the new tenets, the king sponsored the capital's metamorphosis into a Buddhist centre. Mahinda himself became so caught up in this religious fervour that when he returned to India he convinced his father Ashoka to part with the right collarbone of the Buddha, which a messenger took back to Anuradhapura to be enshrined in Lanka's first stupa.

According to the *Mahavamsa* (The Great Lineage), a mixture of fact and legend that served as Sri Lanka's primary historical text prior to European colonisation, the Buddha himself made three visits to Lanka during his mid-6th-century BC life span. Once the Buddha's collarbone had arrived with Ashokan emissaries roughly 300 years later, King Devanampiya Tissa decided to build Anuradhapura's first stupa on a spot where the Buddha supposedly propounded Buddhist philosophy on his third and final trip to Lanka.

ABOVE *This slab carved with a* naga, *the seven-headed serpent considered a guardian of Buddhism, was found at the Abhayagiri Dagaba.*

BELOW *Semicircular 'moonstones' (so called by early Western historians because the centre was thought to resemble a half-moon) were placed just outside entry ways to stupa promenades and may have symbolised movement towards nirvana. Originally these inscribed slabs featured a creeper around the empty centre, followed by a ring of horses and one of elephants, then more foliage and a lotus, symbolising transmigration and gradual emancipation. Later the bull and lion were added, the four animals together taken to stand for the four cardinal directions. This particular example goes a step further by adding a layer of* hamsa, *the brahminy duck sacred to Hindu-Buddhist traditions.*

OPPOSITE *King Devanampiya Tissa ordered the construction of the Thuparama Dagaba during his 250–210 BC reign, and it is as old or older than any stupa now visible in India. Said to enshrine the Buddha's right collarbone – a gift from India's King Ashoka – the stupa has been renovated more than once. Its current form dates to 1862.*

Although we know little about any preparations, consecrations or other ceremonies that may have been organised in the early stages of construction, the chronicles claim that when the monarch deposited the bone in the Thuparama Dagaba's relic chamber, around 220 BC, 'a terrific earthquake was produced, making the hair of the spectators stand on end'. Thuparama, although not Sri Lanka's largest stupa, is still the island's most venerated due to its age and relic content. Devout Theravada Buddhists everywhere regard it as one of the most sacred sites in the world today.

The now classic design features a two-stage plinth ascended by two sets of steps, each fronted by a 2m semicircular carved stone slab. Carved with lotus and animal motifs, and usually referred to as 'moonstones' because of their half-moon shapes, such slabs are found nowhere else and hence appear to be a native feature of Lankan religious architecture.

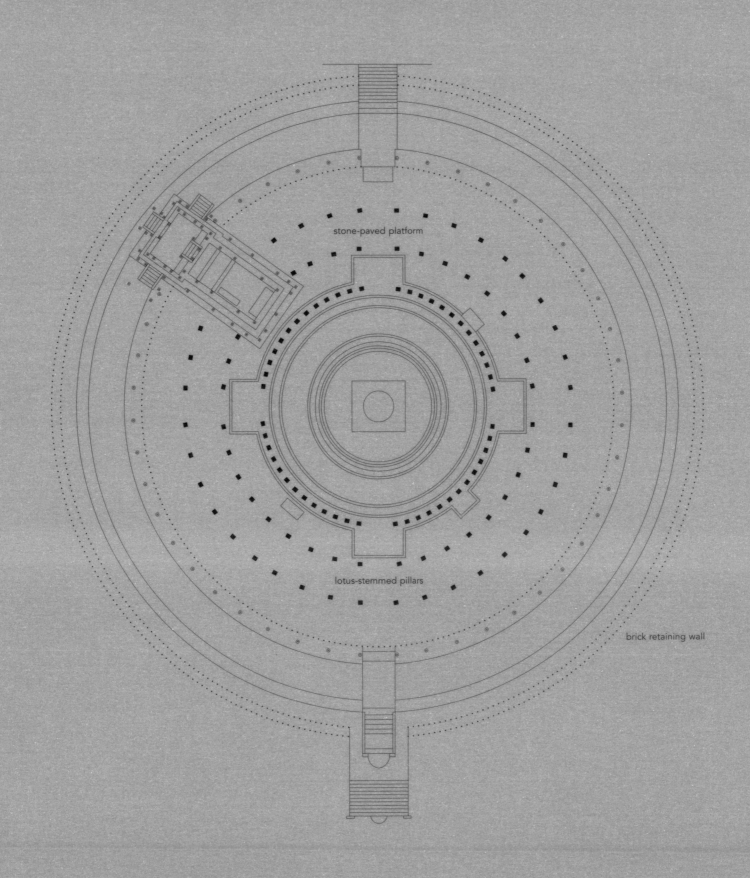

stone-paved platform

lotus-stemmed pillars

brick retaining wall

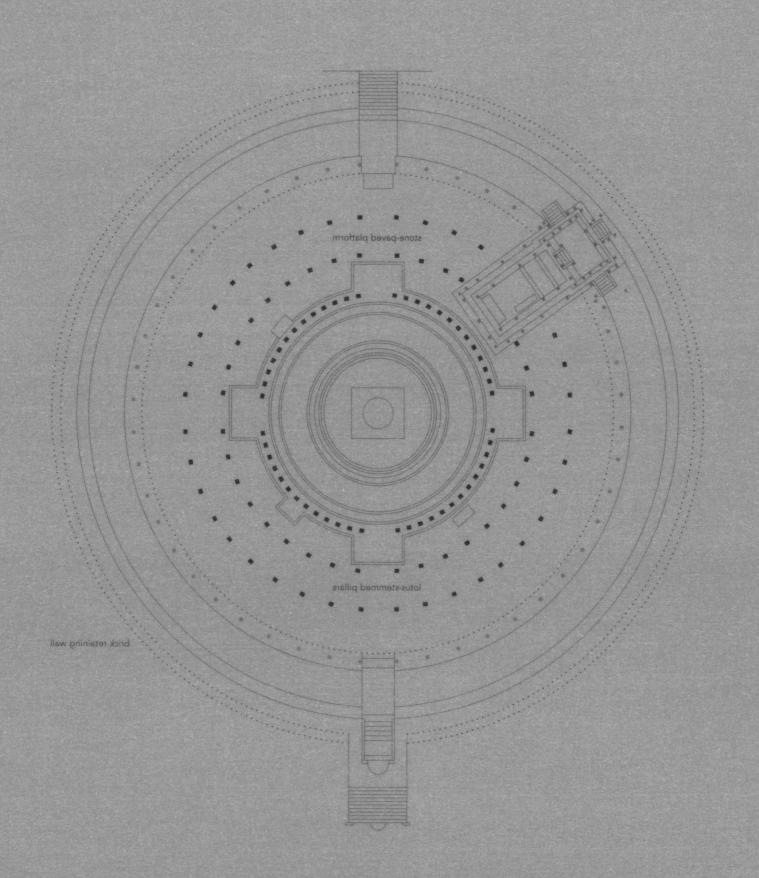

Measuring 12.35m in diameter at its base, the stupa's bell-shaped *anda*, or dome, supports a cube-shaped *harmika* topped by a ribbed cone and a crystal *chattravali*, or umbrella, for a total base-to-tip height of 19m. Like its Indian predecessors, the stupa consists of individually handmade and carefully assembled bricks which have been covered with a thick layer of plaster. Although the pediment is original, most if not all of Thuparama's superstructure dates to an 1862 renovation. Drawings of the original stupa, rendered by a British artist prior to this date, suggest that the simple brick dome was of roughly the same diameter but only about a metre high. Ostensibly this original mound forms part of the stupa's innermost core, and may itself be a brick mantle over earth fill. The entire monument is whitewashed with a lime solution that must be reapplied frequently – usually in preparation for an important festival.

ABOVE *During the full moon festival Sinhalese worshippers come and go from the neatly kept grounds of Ruwanweli Dagaba. Legend has it that it always rains at full moon.*

BELOW *Lions are frequently seen in relief panels from stupas at Anuradhapura. They may have been a reference to the conversion of the Sinhalese by representatives of India's great Buddhist king, Ashoka, who made frequent use of the lion symbol in Buddhist art and architecture produced under his sponsorship. Or they may simply pay homage to the Buddha's courage, leadership qualities and royal lineage. This one was attached to the base of Ruwanweli Dagaba.*

OPPOSITE *Anuradhapura's 82m Ruwanweli Dagaba was constructed during the final years of King Dutthagamani Abhaya's reign (161–137 BC). The* Mahavamsa, *Sri Lanka's most important early historical chronicle, devotes several chapters to the Mahathupa, or Great Stupa, as it was then known. It informs us that, in contrast to the whitewashing popular today, the dome of the stupa was once painted with frescoes.*

Slender, capital-topped pillars, perhaps Thuparama's most unique feature, surround the stupa in four concentric circles. Impressions on the stupa pediments indicate the pillars originally numbered 176, of which 31 still stand complete with capitals, 10 minus their capitals, and 93 lie broken in situ, leaving 42 pillars unaccounted for. Art historians agree that the elegantly designed pillars formed passageways (*peseva* in Sinhalese) for stupa circumambulation. However, scholars hotly debate whether the pillars supported Buddhist sculpture like the Ashokan pillars of India, or whether at one time they may have supported a *vatadage* or wood-and-tile roofed pavilion enclosing the entire stupa and pediment.

King Devanampiya Tissa ordered the construction of a 19m-long *vihara* or Buddhist monastic residence to the south-west of the Thuparama Dagaba, and the ruins still stand today. The tradition of building *viharas* and stupas together became the most classically simple Buddhist monastery plan, one which lives on throughout much of South-East Asia.

Although founded in the 4th century BC, before Buddhism arrived in Sri Lanka, and enduring over 1200 years, Anuradhapura enjoyed perhaps its greatest artistic output under the Buddhist kings of the 3rd century BC and 4th century AD, when temple and stupa architecture flourished.

Seven major stupas pierce the Anuradhapura horizon, each of them a masterpiece of engineering and construction and a testament to the flourishing of Buddhist arts in Sri Lanka. In addition to the oldest, the Thuparama Dagaba, stupa-watchers can still gaze upon the great forms of the Jetavana (Jetavanarama) Dagaba, Ruwanweli (Ruvanvali) Dagaba, Lankarama Dagaba, Mirisaweti (Mirisawati) Dagaba, Abhayagiri Dagaba and Kujjatissa Dagaba.

ABOVE *This elephant relief was found at Mihinthale, the spot where King Ashoka's son Mahinda reportedly converted King Devanampiya Tissa to Buddhism in the 3rd century BC.*

FAR RIGHT *The bases of several of Sri Lanka's earliest stupas bear relief panels depicting a dwarf-like figure thought to be* Kubera, *the Hindu-Buddhist god of wealth.*

BELOW *This relief from Mihinthale depicts a* kalasha, *or vase, symbolising wealth and prosperity.*

OPPOSITE *Scholars disagree as to whether Abhayagiri Dagaba, in Anuradhapura, was built during the reign of King Vattagamini (97–77 BC) or King Gajabahu (AD 114–36). The stupa was probably rebuilt several times to reach its peak 75m height (68m with a broken spire) and 94m base diameter, at which point it probably resembled the fully restored Ruwanweli Dagaba, also in Anuradhapura. Chinese pilgrim Faxian's account of his AD 412 visit to Sri Lanka singled out Abhayagiri for mention, suggesting that by then it must have been very large. The stupa is currently undergoing restoration to remove encroaching vegetation and halt structural decay.*

The basic design of all the seven monuments of Anuradhapura – large hemispheres placed on three-tiered circular terraces, topped by a *harmika* cube and ribbed spire – appears to have been directly inspired by stupas at the 1st to 3rd century AD Buddhist centres of Amaravati and Nagarjunakonda of South India. Except for their impressively laid-out bases, none of the model stupas at Amaravati and Nagarjunakonda survives intact today – a Hindu maharaja dismantled the brick domes to provide material for nearby palace constructions – though elevations of the original designs were carved into stone friezes found at these sites.

ABOVE *The base of the stupa at Yatala Vehara in Tissamaharama, ascribed to the 3rd-century-BC reign of King Yatala Tissa, has been buttressed to slow erosion by ground water. In earlier times the base was adorned with sculpted elephants who appeared to support the stupa.*

BELOW *The stupa at the Raja Maha Vehara in Kelaniya, north of Colombo, follows the standard Sinhalese formula, with a monumental dome topped by a prominent* harmika *and* chattravali. *The Raja Maha Vehara is the second most visited Buddhist temple in Sri Lanka after Kandy's Temple of the Tooth.*

OPPOSITE *Tissamaharama Dagaba, said to have been built by King Kavantissa in the 2nd century BC, bristles with scaffolding used for ongoing renovations.*

One Amaravati relief clearly shows the presence of tall, slender pillars like those at Thuparama. That they appear without any sort of adjoining roof lends credence to the theory that the pillars were not intended to support such a structure. A 3rd-century AD inscription at Nagarjunakonda mentions the donation of a *bodhi-ghara* (carved rail enclosure for a Bodhi tree) to a Sinhalese monastery, thus confirming the connection between Lanka and these centres.

A 10th-century Indian invasion interrupted the Lankan monarchical succession as well as the Buddhist ordination lineage. It wasn't until AD 1066, the same year as the Norman invasion of England, that a new Lankan kingdom was created at Polonnaruwa, about 80km south-east of Anuradhapura in the Mahaweli Ganga valley. Here developed the *pañchavasa*, or 'five dwelling' monastery plan, consisting of a Buddha image shrine, Bodhi tree shrine, chapter house (monks' residence), *uposatha* (ordination hall) and *sabha* (assembly hall) and, of course, a stupa enshrining the monastery's most sacred relics. As at Anuradhapura, stupa architects fitted a brick mantle over earth fill to create the stupa domes, which mounted large square or circular bases. The domes were topped by cube-like *harmikas* and grooved, conical spires.

ABOVE *Dwarfs — possibly representations of Kubera — support a balustrade at the Vatadage in Polonnaruwa.*

RIGHT *The multitiered Satmahal Prasada in Polonnaruwa resembles the Chedi Kukut, a stepped stupa built in Lamphun, Thailand, around the same time (see page 80). One of the main differences between the two monuments is that the Satmahal Prasada features only one Buddha niche on each side of each level, while Chedi Kukut bears multiple niches.*

BELOW *Kiri Vehara, the best preserved unrestored stupa at Polonnaruwa, still retains most of its original plaster. This stupa dates to the 11th- to 13th-century era when Polonnaruwa served as Lanka's capital.*

OPPOSITE *The 54m Rankot Vehara stupa, the largest in Polonnaruwa and the fourth largest on the island, has been ascribed to the reign of King Nissakamalla (1187–96). Like the other major stupas in Anuradhapura and Polonnaruwa, the dome consists of earth fill covered by a brick mantle and plaster. Here scaffolding allows workers to carry out restoration from the top down.*

Under the Polonnaruwa kings of the 11th and 12th centuries, strong cultural, economic and religious links with Myanmar, Thailand, Cambodia and other South-East Asian kingdoms were established. Learned *bhikkhus* (monks) from Thailand sailed to Sri Lanka to restore Buddhist monasticism on the island. They took back with them much artistic inspiration. Via Thailand, Sinhalese dagabas became the most influential of all stupas in the Theravada Buddhist world.

THE LANGUAGE OF STUPAS

The *Rigveda*, a Brahmanic text thought to have been composed around 1200 BC, contains the earliest known usage of the Sanskrit word 'stupa', where it refers variously to a 'knot or tuft of hair; the upper part of the head; crest, top or summit'.

Giuseppe Tucci, author of the influential 1932 *Stupa Art, Architectonics & Symbolism*, proposed that the stupa's most basic concrete reference was to a vertical pole heaped with straw to create rustic haystacks, an agricultural feature common in South and South-East Asia to this day. In modern Assamese, *thupa* in fact means 'heap of straw'. Across these translations and usages, Tucci noted that the attributes of supremacy (topknot, crest, summit), stability (stem, post, stump) and abundance (heaped or piled) came to the fore.

Alongside the English borrowing of the Sanskrit 'stupa', one finds the synonym 'tope', a word borrowed from Punjabi. The earliest usage of 'tope' to mean 'stupa' in a written English work occurs in the 1839 *Account of the Kingdom of Caubool*, by Mount-Stewart Elphinstone, but the word can also be found as early as 1815, in English texts, to mean 'hat' – particularly native headwear worn during the British Raj. It's likely the French word *toupée* (hairpiece) is related. The word *tope* also occurs in modern Spanish, where it refers to small steel hemispheres – like miniature versions of the Great Stupa at Sanchi – placed in a row across motorways to force drivers to slow down.

Another term appearing in Sanskrit literature, *chaitya* (Pali: *chetiya*), eventually joined 'stupa' in the same realm of reference. Brahmin priests used fire altars known as *chiti*, often made of bricks, to perform the ancient Indic *yajña* or fire sacrifice. An unusually powerful *chiti* might evolve over time into a permanent monument dedicated to a particular Hindu deity, in which case it became known as a *chaitya*.

The same may have occurred on the sites of funeral pyres where personages of royal status were cremated following death. The cremation site of a particularly pious, just or respected Hindu raja may have been deemed conducive to the future enactment of rites and rituals associated with Hinduism – as if the raja's spirit lingered on to aid the ceremonies later performed. Royal ashes and bone may also simply have been interred in a separate place in a tumulus or large, rounded earthen mound.

Whether on the former sites of fire altars, royal funeral pyres or royal burial mounds, the main functions of these *chaityas* were to memorialise and pay tribute to an entity of suprahuman significance, an entity believed to subsist beyond the everyday human sphere. These monuments served as a link between two worlds, the visible and the invisible.

In Nepal *chaitya* is the usual term for 'stupa', although they are also referred to as *chibha* in the local idiom. The Javanese word *chandi* (or *candi*) probably derives from *chaitya*, as does the Thai *chedi* or *jedi* and Burmese *zedi* (which refers specifically to solid stupas as distinct from *pahto*, hollow stupas for interior circumambulation).

At the root of many terms for stupa is the Pali-Sanskrit *dhatu*, literally meaning 'element'. This refers to the essential element of Buddhism that the stupa enshrines (originally the corporeal relics of the Buddha himself). The Thai and Lao *thâat*, and Vietnamese *thap* (temple) are derivations of this word.

The Sinhalese in Sri Lanka shortened the term *dhatugarbha* – 'element-womb' – to *dagaba* or *dagoba*. Among British colonisers in India, Myanmar and Sri Lanka, the term became 'pagoda' in English. This is a possible transposition of the syllables contained in *dagoba*, although there has also been speculation that 'pagoda' may have come from the Persian *butkadah* (idol temple) or, less convincingly, the Portuguese *pagao* (pagan).

The Burmese *paya* and Thai *phra* refer to both 'stupa' and 'holy person'. Chinese stupas of the Tang dynasty are known as *ta*, (or occasionally *cheti*, from the Pali *chetiya*) and similar stupas in Korea as *t'ap*; both terms probably derive from *dhatu*. The Japanese tower stupa is called *to*, probably from the Chinese *ta*, and thus also a rendering of *dhatu* or 'relic/element'. From this comes the name of the smaller Japanese structure, the *gorinto* (five-element stupa). Gorintos are also less commonly called *sotoba* (from the Sanskrit 'stupa').

The Tibetan word for 'stupa', *chorten*, is a pairing of the Tibetan 'offering' (*mchod*) and 'receptacle' (*rten*).

Near Kasi, in northern Laos, a farmer stands next to a stack of harvested rice ears. Such natural symbols of peace and prosperity may have influenced the development of the stupa.

ENCIRCLING THE STUPA

For Buddhists, the stupa fuses two principal functions. The first involves keeping alive the memory of the great teacher, Gautama Buddha, and his teachings, by providing a focal point for commemorative activities and a container for holy relics. The stupa's second function is to serve as a bond among members of the Buddhist community who view the structure as a potentially powerful instrument for spiritual transformation.

The first purpose is served when Buddhists make simple offerings of flowers, incense and candles at the base of the stupa, typically on the stupa's most auspicious side, the side facing east, the direction from which the sun rises.

The second may be achieved by the ancient Hindu-Buddhist practice of *pradakshina*, walking along the circumference of the stupa in a clockwise direction. Such circumambulations are said to induce a meditative state of mind to better contemplate the *buddhadharma*, and, in some traditions (chiefly Mahayana and Tantric) such actions also accumulate religious merit.

Since at least the construction of the Great Stupa at Sanchi, India, in the 3rd century BC, stupa designs have included brick, stone or tile pathways dedicated to *pradakshina*. At many monumental stupas, such as Pha That Luang in Laos, Borobudur in Java or Thatbyinnyu Pahto in Myanmar, multiple pathways may be found on more than one terrace to encourage multiple circumambulations. Often reliefs, sculpture and other iconography will differ from level to level, thus creating a pedagogic 'spiral' effect as the visitor ascends the terraces.

Typically the worshipper begins at the east side of the stupa and proceeds south, thus following the daily course of the sun from sunrise to zenith, sunset and nadir. In some cultures, moving in the opposite direction, anticlockwise *(prashavya)*, may be prescribed for funeral ceremonies.

Followers of the pre-Buddhist Bön tradition in Tibet also regularly perform their circumambulations in reverse, as do certain followers of esoteric Tantrism. This is known as the 'left-hand path', in part because the circuit keeps the left side of the worshipper's body towards the stupa or other sacred site.

In Theravada Buddhist cultures, stupa circumambulations are reserved for certain holidays in the Buddhist calendar and are thus not regularly performed every time a stupa is visited. A Theravada Buddhist walks three rounds in homage to the 'Triple Gems' of the Buddha, Dharma and Sangha.

In Himalayan lands, where stupa circumambulation is often referred to by the Tibetan term *kora*, the practice is considered so crucial to one's spiritual development that pilgrims may perform thousands of circumambulations around sacred sites in a lifetime. In addition to stupas, these may include monasteries, cities, even entire mountains. The *kora* takes on added potency when a particularly ardent devotee performs a full prostration with every step.

A lone monk performs kora *around a simple but solid stupa in Sakya, Tibet.*

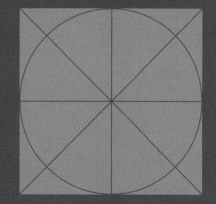

ISLAND STUPAS

OPPOSITE *Stairways and stepped gates*
link the open passageways through
Borobudur's nine ascending terraces.

ISLAND STUPAS

BOROBUDUR

When Thomas Stamford Raffles and his crew of surveyors working for the British Empire first spotted a large, oddly symmetrical, dome-shaped hill in central Java in 1814, little did they know it covered one of Asia's greatest artistic achievements. What they were to discover would shatter their assumptions about Java's religious past.

Peering out from amid the hill's thick foliage, smoothly carved stone Buddha figures rocked the colonialists' perspective that Java was an exclusively Islamic domain. As the surveyors dug away the topsoil around the few visible sculptures, we can imagine that the mass of solid stone blocks they found beneath both excited and puzzled. At the time, Java was considered a cultural backwater bereft of monumental art, an island bypassed by the great Indian and Chinese civilisations that had so affected other parts of South-East Asia.

The European rediscovery of Borobudur – called Boro Bodo in Raffles' impressive 1817 *The History of Java* – led historians worldwide to uncover new links between Java and the Indic religious traditions that extended well beyond the usual 'southern route' followed by Buddhism as it moved from India and Sri Lanka to South-East Asia. Although Buddhism appears to have first reached the islands of Sumatra and Java via missionaries in the Theravada monastic tradition, probably in the early Christian centuries, Borobudur and associated monuments in central Java clearly indicate that Tantric Buddhism found its way to the Indonesian archipelago early on.

Java's earliest Buddhist inscription, dating to AD 778, dedicates Chandi Kalasan to Tara, a Tantric Buddhist goddess of some renown in Nepal and Tibet. Although the Tara cult is thought to have originated in north-east India during the Gupta era (3rd to 6th centuries AD), the Kalasan inscription is the earliest known epigraphic reference to the goddess thus far found anywhere in the world. The same inscription states that Chandi Kalasan belonged to the Sailendra kingdom, a Mahayana Buddhist kingdom that encompassed the Thai-Malay Peninsula as well as Sumatra and Java. Scholars today believe the early Sailendra monarchs may have been relatives of India's Chandela dynasty, who sponsored the construction of several Hindu temples, including the famously erotic 10th-century Khajuraho complex. One legend says the ruling clan split between those who followed Tantric Hinduism and remained in India, and those who set off for Java to live as Tantric Buddhists.

Sailendra dynastic power peaked between the 7th and 9th centuries AD, and the kings of Sailendra constructed all of Java's Buddhist sites within a single 70-year span, roughly AD 760 to 830. Of the several Buddhist monuments erected by the Sailendras, Java's Borobudur not only outranks all other Sailendra architecture in scope and size, but also qualifies as the largest Buddhist structure in the world.

Built by order of King Samaratungga – two to three centuries earlier than Cambodia's Angkor Wat or Myanmar's Bagan and nearly half a millennium before architects began planning the great cathedrals of Europe – Borobudur represents perhaps the greatest single achievement in the history of Buddhist art. Although Java has long since ceased to be a Buddhist centre and relatively few Buddhists visit Borobudur, the stupa has become one of Indonesia's most esteemed tourist attractions.

Like all stupas, Borobudur's overall form represents both mountain and mandala. In Hindu-Buddhist cosmology Mt Meru (or Sumeru) sits at the centre of the universe, surrounded by concentric circles or squares representing seven continents alternating with cosmic oceans. Two-dimensional elevation sketches of the mythical land form – in temple murals and illustrated Buddhist manuscripts, for example – look very stupa-like.

Both Mt Meru and its architectural representation, the stupa, follow a symmetrical plan which, when seen from above, forms a mandala. Mandalas, elaborate diagrams created by Buddhist artists as objects for visual or internal contemplation, typically feature four gates leading inward to three or more concentric levels, with a main deity in the centre surrounded by other deities at the perimeters of each level. The mandala's precise geometry of circles, squares and axes placed in measured space, is further elaborated by iconographic elements such as the lotus, the *vajra* (thunderbolt), clouds, water and a whole pantheon of Buddhist deities.

So influential has the mountain-mandala concept been in the Buddhist cultures of South-East Asia that palaces, cities and even entire kingdoms were once physically organised in a Meru- and mandala-like manner, with the temporal ruler at the centre and vassals and subjects at the perimeters.

Although all stupas project a mandala-like plan if viewed from above, Borobudur's low profile – some observers have likened it to a flattened or badly risen cake – makes this aspect of the design much more evident than usual. Many scholars believe the architects of Borobudur designed the monument to evoke the most important mandala in Tantric Buddhism, the Vajradhatu (Diamond Element) mandala.

According to Tantric Buddhist tradition, Mahavairochana – the Great Illuminator via whom all Buddhas are enlightened – sits at both the centre of the Vajradhatu mandala and on the summit of Mt Meru. The geometry of most stupas focuses on one aspect over the other, but in Borobudur we find a perfect balance between mountain and mandala. Here the Buddhist devotee was able to ascend the mountain while at the same time circumambulating each level of the mandala, moving from the world of desire in the lower terraces to the world of formlessness at the top.

Borobudur's Vital Statistics
Narrative reliefs: 1460
Decorative reliefs: 1212
Buddhas in niches: 432
Buddhas in small stupas: 72
Decorated gateways: 24
Number of carved stone blocks:
around a million

Borobudur's Vital Statistics

Narrative reliefs: 1460

Decorative reliefs: 1212

Buddhas in niches: 432

Buddhas in small stupas: 72

Decorated gateways: 24

Number of carved stone blocks: around a million

Photograph: Luca Tettoni

Beneath Borobudur's earthen mantle Raffles' archaeologists found 6500 cubic metres of carved stone meticulously arranged to transmit Buddhist lessons to the faithful. The mandala plan, though complex in its specifics, essentially represents the Buddhist's journey from ignorance to wisdom. The stupa's nine ascending terraces – six lower terraces square in overall shape and three upper ones arranged in concentric circles – are joined by stairways and stepped gates. Connected by stone passageways, these lead the visitor in a spiral-like climb up the monument, one stage at a time, along a designated route through the mandala.

As visitors wend their way through the ascending passageways to the 34.5m summit, their view of the terraces above and below is blocked, reinforcing the idea that the whole of life cannot be understood till the journey has ended. Along the way the passageways provide plenty of opportunity for spiritual development via 1460 exquisitely carved stone relief panels illustrating five Buddhist texts, in ascending order: *Mahakarmavibhanga* (The Great Discrimination of Actions), *Jatakamala* (Garland of Birth Stories), *Lalitavistara* (Unfolding of the Play), *Gandavyuha* (Structure of the World Compared to a Bubble) and *Bhadrachari* (Samantabhadra's Vow).

Unlike the dry text found in the palm-leaf manuscripts of 8th-century Buddhist Asia, or the straightforward single layer of reliefs found on dome-shaped Indian or bell-shaped Lankan stupas, Borobudur's carved stone panels represent a complex matrix of didactic art. Between the earthy images of profane worldliness found at the lowermost level and the austere, dignified portrayals of Buddhist enlightenment gracing the upper levels, a considerable effort must be spent to take in everything the stupa offers. In fact to view every relief panel will require 10 circuits – four along the lowermost level and two each along the three upper galleries – for a distance of 1200m.

That's only the beginning of the journey. Ascending from the last of the four levels of square terraces onto the three circular levels, the teaching content undergoes a striking transformation as the pilgrim moves symbolically closer to nirvana. Here one is confronted by 72 bell-shaped stupas, each containing a life-size stone Buddha peering outward from the monument through square perforations in the stupa domes. Although they are invisible to pilgrims climbing the monument, an additional 432 stone Buddha images – 108 on each of the four sides – are placed in exterior niches along the lower square terraces.

The three upper levels allow unobstructed views of the surrounding Kedu Plain, perhaps symbolising the sense of mental spaciousness attained in the final stages of Buddhist psychospiritual evolution. At the summit, a large central stupa once contained a stone Buddha probably meant to represent Mahavairochana, considered the Great Illuminator or eternal Buddha in Tantric Buddhism. The image, the carving of which was never completed, was found lying 100m from Borobudur. Before historians concluded that this image originally belonged in the uppermost stupa, popular theory suggested the empty stupa evoked the emptiness of nirvana.

Around 2km east of Borobudur stand Chandi Pawon and Chandi Mendut, two Buddhist monuments of the same archaeological vintage as Borobudur. Mendut, the larger of the two, is said to be a representation of Tantric Buddhism's Garbhadhatu (Womb Element) mandala and contains several venerable Buddhas. Although not in everyday worship, Chandi Mendut serves as focus for much Indonesian Buddhist celebration during the annual Vesakha Puja festival, which honours the birth, enlightenment and death of the Buddha and usually falls in May. Before Borobudur attained Unesco World Heritage Site status, the Buddhist faithful organised a colourful procession from Mendut to Borobudur during Vesakha.

JAVA'S CHANDIS

ABOVE *Chandi Sari exhibits a unique tri-fold symmetry with three main levels, three statuary chambers and three stupa finials.*

LEFT *A relief panel depicting the Bodhisattva Avalokiteshvara at Chandi Plaosan.*

BELOW *A similar image of Avalokiteshvara at Chandi Sari.*

OPPOSITE *Rotund guardian deities watch over the promenade to Chandi Sewu, second largest Buddhist complex in Java after Borobudur.*

The second-largest Buddhist complex in Java after Borobudur, Chandi Sewu, consisted of 249 *chandis* believed to have been constructed in the mid-to-late 8th century AD. Designed on a mandala plan and, like Borobudur, assembled from carved volcanic andesite, the main temple at Sewu formed a 20-cornered polygon that once stood 30m high and measured 29m in diameter. The temple was dedicated to Manjushri, the Tantric Buddhist deity of the power of wisdom. Though smaller in scale, Chandi Plaosan to the east of Sewu was a similar assemblage of inspiring shrines, temples and stupas. Ornamentation combined both Buddhist and Hindu symbols, perhaps reflecting the overlap of two dynastic sponsors, the Buddhist Sailendra (King Samaratungga) and Hindu Sanjaya (King Rakai Pikatan).

North-west of Yogyakarta lies a cluster of several more Buddhist monuments of similar age and style. Chandi Kalasan, the most impressive, was dedicated to the Tantric Buddhist goddess Tara and is the earliest known Tantric Buddhist monument associated with the saviour goddess. Standing 6m tall, Kalasan was once surrounded by 52 stupas.

LEFT *A statue of Lokeshvara inside Chandi Plaosan.*

BELOW *This lone finial lying near Goa Gajah may be the only visible evidence that Buddhist architecture once existed on the island of Bali.*

OPPOSITE *Artisans assembled Chandi Plaosan from carved volcanic andesite blocks. The rising terrace levels of Borobudur have been compacted into cuboid bases, topped by dense stupa clusters.*

The short-lived Javanese Buddhist empire, though it had scarce lasting effect on Javanese culture, did manage to play an important role in the transmission of Buddhism to other parts of Asia. Atisha, a famous Buddhist scholar from Bengal, may have studied Tantric Buddhism with an Indonesian master for a number of years before travelling to Tibet, where he established an enduring Tibetan Buddhist lineage. As one Tibetan chronicle reports:

Here in Tibet, five traditions have come down to us…Among these, the most distinguished is the school of Atisha: both he and his own teacher Dharmakirti of the Golden Isles [Java and Sumatra] continually saw the face of the Holy Lady [Tara], and upon them was bestowed the tradition.

A Javanese monk is also reported to have travelled to Tang dynasty China, where he instructed Kobo Daishi (AD 774–835), who later founded the Shingon or 'True Word' sect of Buddhism in Japan. Java's Sailendra monarchs enjoyed much influence in 8th- to 9th-century Cambodia as well.

Ironically Buddhism's Indonesian era – perhaps a linchpin in the spread of Tantric Buddhism to Tibet, China and Japan – has been almost entirely forgotten in its native land.

GOLDEN LANDS

OPPOSITE *The Dai, an Austro-Thai ethnic minority in south-western China, built the Manfeilong Ta near Damenglong in 1203. Like most Buddhists in Thailand, Laos and Myanmar, the Dai follow Theravada Buddhism, and this stupa shares structural and decorative elements with typical stupa designs found in these 'golden lands'. Because the 16m central stupa and its eight satellite stupas resemble a cluster of bamboo shoots, it is known locally as the Bamboo Shoot Stupa.*

Around the 1st century AD, according to Cambodian legend, an Indian noble called Kaundinya arrived on the shores of mainland South-East Asia as commanded in a dream. Wielding a sacred lance, he conquered the new land and married Soma, a Cambodian queen said to be half human, half serpent. Together they established a kingdom on a hilltop along the southern reach of the Mekong River in what today comprises southern Cambodia. Although the facts are obscured by myth, this story – of which there are several regional variations – symbolises a general truth accepted by scholars today, that Indian immigrants to South-East Asia intermarried with the natives and created a new culture.

This culture laid Indian religion and art over indigenous custom in a way that fused the two traditions into one. Perhaps much as 'westernisation' is affecting South-East Asia today – making Ronald McDonald a universally recognised figure – the 'Indianisation' of Asia west of the Annamite Mountains franchised Shiva and Buddha.

Cambodians knew the first Indianised kingdom as Phnom, Khmer for 'hill' or 'mountain'. The Chinese, who were the first and only outsiders to write about this era in South-East Asian history, Sinicised the name as Funan. Essentially no architecture from the Funan empire remains, but since Hinduism appears to have dominated Funan, it's unlikely any Buddhist monuments were erected.

Burmese and Thai chronicles assert that during the 3rd century BC, India's King Ashoka sent Buddhist missionaries east to a land called Suvannabhumi (Golden Land). Suvannabhumi most likely corresponds to a remarkably fertile area stretching from southern Myanmar, across central Thailand, including what is now Laos, to western Cambodia. If these early Buddhist visitors sponsored or inspired stupa construction, none has ever been verifiably documented, despite regional legends claiming that certain present-day stupas – such as Thailand's Phra Pathom Chedi – were built over stupas dating to this period. However, there seems little doubt that by the 1st century AD, Buddhism had accompanied Indian traders to mainland South-East Asia, and as Buddhism became accepted locally, stupas followed.

GOLDEN LANDS

The earliest visible Buddhist architecture in mainland South-East Asia dates to the 6th century AD, after the collapse of the Funan empire. Around this time a people known as the Pyu – possibly hailing from the Tibeto-Burman plateau – created city-states in what is today central Myanmar. Epigraphs from the 5th or 6th centuries AD indicate the Pyu had frequent contact with eastern India, and the art and architecture left behind suggest they practised Mahayana Buddhism mixed with Hinduism.

LEFT The almost cylindrical Bawbawgyi, near the present-day town of Pyay, is thought to have been built by the Pyu civilisation between the 5th and 9th centuries AD. It may have been one of four similar stupas that delineated the four corners of the Pyu capital Thayekhittaya (Sri Ksetra).

ABOVE RIGHT The sharply conical Payagyi may have been another of the four 'sentry stupas' at Thayekhittaya.

BELOW A monk meditates at the foot of Payagyi.

OPPOSITE Ananda Pahto, one of the most striking archaeological remains from the Bagan era, forms a virtual mountain of stupas. Thought to have been erected in 1105, its hollow centre of cavernous circumambulatory chambers is topped by a stupa-like tower standing 51m above the ground. Smaller stupas adorn every major corner of the monument and mount each of the entry ways as well as the numerous niches found on each level.

MYANMAR

Between the 5th and 9th centuries AD, the Pyu built the earliest known stupas in Myanmar, and the oldest stupas still standing anywhere in South-East Asia, at Thayekhittaya (known in Sanskrit as 'Sri Ksetra'). Four tall, round-topped, almost cylindrical stupas – built of brick and standing on round bases – marked the cardinal points of the Pyu kingdom. Three – Payagyi, Bawbawgyi and Payama – can be seen today near the village of Hmawza.

Around this same time, the Mon developed the fertile lowlands stretching from the Ayeyarwady River delta across Thailand to western Cambodia. Several major stupas in Myanmar, including Shwedagon, claim to be built on the site of much older Mon stupas.

LEFT *At 114m, Shwemawdaw Paya dominates the skyline of Bago, a former Mon capital. Said to have been built over an older 23m Mon stupa in 1796, a succession of earthquakes in the 19th and early 20th centuries severely damaged the monument. It was entirely rebuilt in the 1950s.*

BELOW *A vendor at Kyaiktiyo offers brass bells to pilgrims who buy them to donate for use in the* hti *(umbrella) atop stupa spires. Thin copper sheets in the shape of bodhi tree leaves catch the wind, producing a delightful tinkling sound.*

BOTTOM *An attendant affixes tiny temple bells to a satellite stupa perched on a vertical boulder at Kyaiktiyo. Worshippers place the bells inside a small cart-like container which is then pulled along a wire to the stupa.*

OPPOSITE *Buddhists in Myanmar consider this gilded boulder, balanced on the edge of a mountain cliff and topped with a 7m, Mon-style stupa, to be the second most sacred site in the country after the Shwedagon Paya in Yangon. Legend says the boulder, known as Kyaiktiyo, is held in place by a hair of the Buddha enshrined in the stupa.*

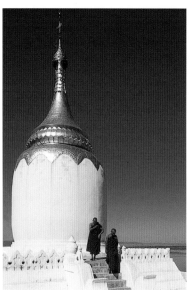

Enter the Burmans, who came south into Myanmar from somewhere in the eastern Himalayas around the 8th or 9th century AD. After the Pyu kingdom was broken up by a Yunnanese invasion in AD 832, the Burmans inherited a spot nestled in a bend in the Ayeyarwady River and gradually initiated the grandest stupa-building campaign seen before or since. Excavations along the ruined city walls indicate that by the end of the 9th century the city had reached complex proportions. Pali inscriptions of the time called the city Arimaddanapura (City of the Enemy Crusher) and Tambadipa (Copper Land), but outsiders knew it as Bagan.

When the devoutly Buddhist King Anawrahta ascended the Bagan throne in 1044, his dissatisfaction with the practice of Buddhism among his subjects led him to seek outside examples of 'proper' Buddhist culture to draw from. Admiring the strict Theravada Buddhism of the Mon at Thaton, a thriving port in southern Myanmar, he conquered Thaton and carried back to Bagan 32 sets of the *Tripitaka* (the Theravada Buddhist canon), the city's monks and scholars and the Mon king himself, King Manuha.

To reinforce the new brand of Buddhism, Anawrahta commenced an ambitious building program. Among the better-known Bagan monuments he constructed are the conical Shwezigon Paya, considered a prototype for all later Burmese stupas; the Pitaka Taik, built to house the scriptures carried back from Thaton on the backs of 30 elephants; and the elegant and distinctive Shwesandaw Paya, built immediately after the conquest of Thaton. Thus began what the Burmese call the First Burmese Empire, which became a major centre for Theravada Buddhism and a destination for Buddhist pilgrims from throughout South-East Asia.

Standing on three diminishing terraces and decorated with floral patterns, this 11th-century bell-shaped Bagan stupa became a virtual prototype for stupas throughout Myanmar.

Standing on three diminishing
terraces and decorated with
floral patterns, this 11th-century
bell-shaped Bagan stupa became
a virtual prototype for stupas
throughout Myanmar.

Anawrahta's successors continued this phenomenal proliferation of stupas and monasteries, which altogether lasted two and a half centuries. Marco Polo described the city-state in his famous 1298 chronicle:

The towers are built of fine stone; and then one of them has been covered with gold a good finger in thickness, so that the tower looks as if it were all of solid gold; and the other is covered with silver in like manner so that it seems to be all of solid silver…they… form one of the finest sights in the world, so exquisitely finished are they, so splendid and costly. And when they are lighted up by the sun they shine most brilliantly and are visible from a vast distance.

The Travels of Marco Polo

Historians disagree on exactly what happened to cause Bagan's apparent rapid decline at the end of the 13th century, but an invasion or threat of invasion by Mongols from the north led to the tearing down of religious monuments to build fortifications, and finally to complete abandonment of the city. Today the remains of some 4000 stupas are visible at Bagan. How many more may once have stood here is difficult to estimate, though Burmese accounts suggesting there were once over four million stupas and shrines can be dismissed, as one scholar put it, as 'the product of poetic effusion'.

Some of the earliest stupa sites at Bagan may in fact predate King Anawrahta, including Ngakywenadaung Paya, Lawkananda Paya and Bupaya Paya, all of which might have originally been erected by the Pyu and restored by the Burmans. Later the Burmans went beyond the classic solid, conical stupa planted on a set of low terraces. They expanded the base into large cuboid structures and placed the more slender sections of the stupa on top. As at 9th-century Buddhist *chandi* sites in central Java and early Buddhist monuments at Angkor, they may have borrowed temple designs from north-east India's Pala era. Indian architects called the cube-like lower structure a *prasada*, while the spire-like superstructure was termed a *shikhara*.

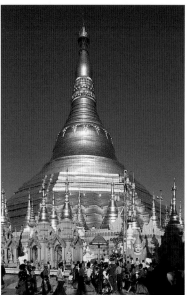

LEFT *Said to have been built over a Mon stupa dating to the 11th century or earlier, the 98m Shwedagon Paya assumed its current form in 1769 after several renovations. During the colonial era, the British military occupied the stupa grounds for 77 years, much to the sorrow of a people for whom this stupa is the holiest religious site in the country. The stupa became an important focal point for the post-WWII independence movement, and again during the 1988 demonstrations against the Union of Burma military regime. Today worshippers throng the tiled walkway around the stupa at all times of day, but the five-hectare grounds also contain many smaller stupas, along with statues, shrines and open pavilions.*

The Burmese language today distinguishes between solid stupas, which are called *zedi*, and those with interior space, the *pahto*. One of the main Burman innovations was to add hollow corridors in the *prasada* section of the stupas to facilitate the circumambulation of the enshrined relics and in some cases to allow worshippers to ascend to raised terraces for further circuits. While Java's Borobudur channels pilgrims through open-air walled corridors, Bagan's great stupas feature completely covered, almost tunnel-like walkways.

BELOW *Green tile and glass mosaic glitter in the sun on this 19th-century stupa at Inwa, the Shan capital of Myanmar from 1364 to 1841. In Shan Buddhist culture, the rabbit symbolises peace as well as the moon.*

OPPOSITE *Rudyard Kipling called the Shwedagon Paya 'a golden mystery… a beautiful winking wonder'.*

Such hollow stupas at Bagan contain a central pillar or shaft where relics are enshrined, with four Buddhas facing out from the pillar. There is typically one corridor around the pillar, linked to straight corridors radiating out along the cardinal points. The walls of such interior spaces are usually filled with colourful murals, either *jatakas* (stories from the life of the Buddha) or Buddha figures displaying various *mudras* (symbolic hand gestures).

After the fall of Bagan, the Shan ruled much of central Myanmar out of Inwa (Ava) from the 14th to 19th centuries. The strictly Theravada Shan created their own stupa style, one which favoured the more traditional cone or bell shapes inherited from Sri Lanka but in a much slimmer, more delicate form.

LEFT *Mandalay's Eindawya Paya, erected in 1847, exhibits the classic Mandalay style in a blend of Burman and Shan influences.*

BELOW *A heavily gilded 19th-century Buddha occupies a mirror-mosaic shrine in a stupa at Sandamani Paya, Mandalay. In the famous Rakhaing style (named for the region in western Myanmar where the style originated), the image bears kingly regalia, a reference to the historical Buddha's royal birth. The crown bears an uncanny resemblance to a stupa spire.*

OPPOSITE *Beginning in 1790, thousands of slaves and prisoners of war laboured to erect Mingun Paya, near the banks of the Ayeyarwady River north of Mandalay, under orders from King Bodawpaya. Construction halted in 1819 when the king died, leaving a massive brick base that stands only a third of its intended 150m height. An 1838 earthquake cracked the walls.*

The religious fervour that yielded thousands of stupas at Bagan and Inwa has become generalised to all of Buddhist Myanmar in modern times. Hardly a day goes by when a new stupa isn't being erected, or an old one being restored somewhere in the country, as Burmese Buddhists continue to believe the sponsorship or building of a stupa to be one of the most meritorious acts a layperson can perform. According to Burmese custom, building a stupa in fact entitles one to be called a *paya-dagagyi* (honoured stupa-builder, male form) or *paya-dagamagyi* (honoured stupa-builder, female form), conferring social as well as spiritual distinction.

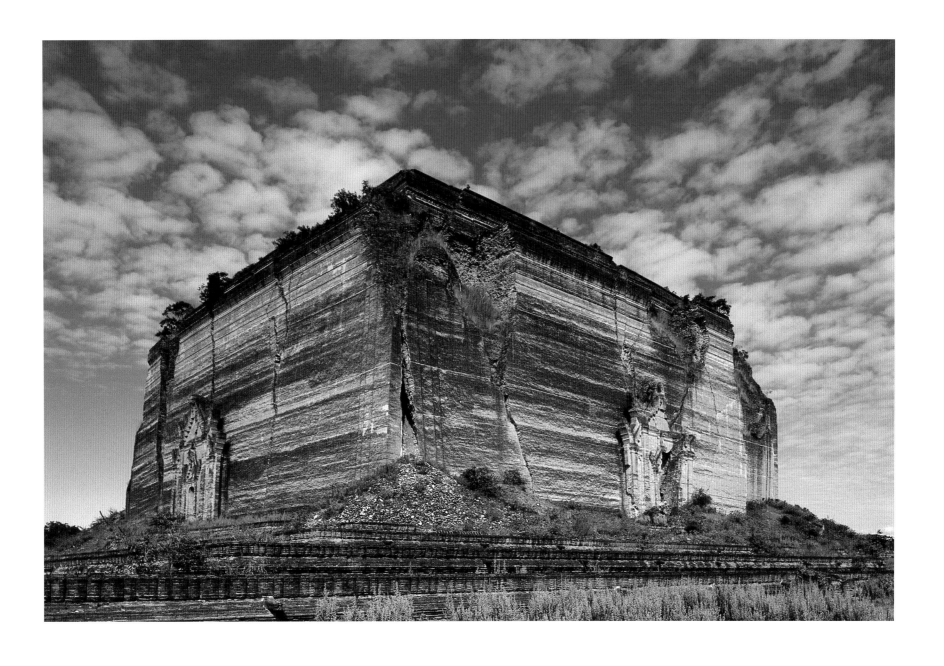

BELOW LEFT *Said to have been partially modelled after Sri Lanka's Mahathupa, Kaunghmudaw Paya near Sagaing stands 46m high and was built in 1636 to commemorate the founding of Inwa, the royal capital of a powerful Shan dynasty.*

BOTTOM *A cluster of whitewashed stupas in Sagaing form the most important religious centre in Myanmar.*

OPPOSITE *Stupa spires of Sagaing pierce the horizon along the Ayeyarwady River.*

BELOW LEFT *Built in 1535 by King Minbin, the most powerful of the Rakhaing kings, Shittaung Paya vaguely resembles Java's Borobudur with its 'flattened cake' outline topped by rows of domed stupas. The maze-like interior corridors of Shittaung are thought to have been used for Tantric Buddhist initiations, much like the terraced walkways of Borobudur, although the two monuments were built nearly 700 years apart.*

BOTTOM *Laymyetnha Paya echoes the strong, bunker-like designs of Dukkanthein and Shittaung Paya.*

OPPOSITE *Fortress-like Dukkanthein in Mrauk U, near the Myanmar-Bangladesh border, consists of thick stone-block terraces topped by round-topped stupas. It is said to have been constructed in 1571 at the height of the Rakhaing kingdom, where a mixture of Theravada and Tantric Buddhism, Brahmanism, Islam and animism was officially endorsed.*

While the royal survivors of the Funan empire appear to have fled to Java, possibly fusing blood lines that led to Java's Sailendra dynasty 300 years later (see Chapter 3, Island Stupas), a new kingdom formed along the lower Mekong River from southern Laos into north-western Cambodia. Known to the Chinese as Chenla, this state flourished from the 6th to 9th centuries and appears to have been Hindu.

CAMBODIA

The powerful Sailendras of Java, with their satellites in Sumatra and Malaya, became very influential in the late 8th and early 9th centuries when they made regular military forays into areas now encompassed by parts of Laos, Cambodia and Vietnam. It's possible that the Sailendras occupied Chenla during the 9th century and influenced the artistic as well as political development of pre-Angkor Cambodia.

LEFT *A relief of dancing apsaras, or heavenly beings, adorns a stone slab at the Bayon in Angkor Thom. Although this temple features both Hindu and Buddhist elements, its 54 towers are carved with the face of the Bodhisattva Avalokiteshvara.*

BELOW *At Udong, the capital of Cambodia from 1618 to 1866, stands a stupa adorned with garlands and, between dome and finial, Buddha faces oriented toward the four cardinal directions.*

OPPOSITE *Erected in 1980, this stupa at Wat Preah Keo Morakot in Phnom Penh contains the ashes of King Norodom Ranariddh, the father of Cambodian King Norodom Sihanouk. Stylistically it is reminiscent of late Ayuthaya or early Bangkok stupas, supplemented by the Cambodian innovation of garland reliefs on the stupa dome.*

As Chenla disintegrated in the 9th century, Jayavarman II, who was educated in the art of kingship at the Sailendra court in Java, came to the fore. From his capital called Hariharalaya (at present-day Roluos near Siem Reap), Jayavarman II reigned approximately AD 800 to 850 and introduced Cambodia to the *devaraja* or 'divine king' cult, which posited the monarch as the worldly representative of the Hindu deities Shiva and Vishnu. Jayavarman II was also the first in Cambodia to build pyramid-shaped monuments of brick or stone, possibly influenced by the Hindu-Buddhist monuments of central Java. Over the next 350 years, under a succession of Khmer devarajas, this style of architecture evolved into the sophisticated set of walled and moated temple complexes known collectively as 'Angkor'.

While in the beginning Hinduism held sway over the ruling strata of society, several Khmer monarchs along the way adopted Mahayana Buddhism. Although few of the monuments they produced, even during the Buddhist periods, can be considered stupas in the classic sense, many shared features with the Pala-influenced stupas of central Java. Tapered towers representing the mythical Mt Meru are common among Angkor-period temple architecture, for example. Ascending sets of diminishing terraces, echoing Borobudur, are also present.

Thailand arguably contains the greatest variety of stupa styles of any country in Asia. As an important commercial and transport relay point between India and Cambodia to the west and east, and between China in the north and the Malay-Indonesian archipelago to the south, the area now occupied by the Thai nation was crisscrossed with religious and cultural influences from many differing sources.

THAILAND

LEFT The stepped, niched design of Chedi Suwan Chang Kot (more popularly known as Chedi Kukut) in Lamphun, Thailand, may have been influenced by Sri Lanka's unique Satmahal Prasada (see page 40). The Mon kingdom of Hariphunchai constructed this stupa in 1218, possibly on top of an earlier 8th- or 9th-century Mon stupa.

BELOW *The 20 whitewashed stupas at Wat Chedi Sao display a blend of Lanna and Shan styles.*

OPPOSITE *The 82m* prang *(Khmer-style tower) of Wat Arun in Bangkok was constructed during the first half of the 19th century. The unique design elongates the typical Khmer* prang *into a distinctly Thai shape. The plaster covering of the brick core is embedded with a mosaic of broken, multihued Chinese porcelain, a common temple ornamentation in the early Ratanakosin period when Chinese ships calling at Bangkok used loads of old porcelain as ballast.*

The central stupa at Wat Arun represents Mt Meru, while the four corner stupas symbolise the four corner continents in the cosmic ocean of the Hindu-Buddhist universe.

The central stupa at Wat Arun
represents Mt Meru, while the
four corner stupas symbolise
the four corner continents in the
cosmic ocean of the Hindu-
Buddhist universe.

During the Angkor period in the far north of Thailand, Thai tribes gathered together in ever-stronger city-states called *meuang*. The decline of Angkor in the mid-13th century allowed these principalities to unite to create Sukhothai (Rising of Happiness) in the lower north. Later the Thais took Hariphunchai from the Mon, and in 1296 joined with rulers in other Thai states, including Luang Prabang and Vientiane, to form Lan Na Thai (literally 'million Thai rice fields'), today often referred to simply as Lanna.

LEFT *North-west of Chiang Mai, on 1676m Doi Suthep, stands Wat Phra That Doi Suthep, established in 1383 under King Keu Naone and one of northern Thailand's most sacred temples. Inside the cloister, this octagonal, Lanna-style, copper-plated chedi is topped by a five-tiered gold umbrella.*

BELOW LEFT *Chiang Mai legend says that the simple but striking Chedi Khao or 'White Stupa' marks the spot where a local man saved Chiang Mai from invasion. According to the story, Uncle Piang volunteered to compete with a diving expert from the invading force to see who could stay under the adjacent Ping River the longest. An expectant crowd marvelled as the champion diver stayed underwater for four minutes, then came gasping to the river's surface. As the citizenry cheered, Piang was declared the winner and Chiang Mai, so the story goes, kept its sovereignty. When Piang didn't surface for several more minutes, the king ordered some of his subjects into the river to search for him. They found his body at the bottom of the river, his sarong tied to a stake.*

BOTTOM *Lanna-style Chedi Luang, dating from 1441, was damaged either by a 16th century earthquake or by the cannon fire of King Taksin in 1775 during the recapture of Chiang Mai from the Burmese. A restoration of the great chedi, financed by Unesco and the Japanese government, stopped short of creating a new spire, since no-one knows how the original superstructure looked.*

OPPOSITE *A temple worker applies a fresh coat of whitewash to a 14th-century stupa Wat Suan Dok, Chiang Mai.*

LEFT *Seven rows of stupas – chedi or jedi in Thai – mark the ruins of Wat Chedi Jet Thaew, a temple complex built in the late 13th century at Si Satchanalai, Thailand. The tallest chedi features a Sukhothai-style finial shaped like a lotus bud.*

BELOW LEFT *The brick shell of 14th-century Chedi Athit Don Kaew, a remnant of the influential Chiang Saen kingdom on the banks of the Mekong River, has fallen open to reveal a smaller stupa inside. Encasement of older stupas is a practice that dates at least to the 2nd and 3rd centuries BC. In the case of Chedi Athit Don Kaew the encased stupa is today more intact than the newer one.*

BELOW RIGHT *Graceful Sukhothai-style sitting Buddhas, in the earth-touching or bhumisparsa pose, flank the brick and stucco ruins of one of the many stupas at Wat Mahathat, the largest monastery complex at Sukhothai.*

OPPOSITE *The 45m Lanna-style stupa at Wat Phra That Lampang Luang was raised in 1449 and restored in 1496. Wrapping cloth the colour of Buddhist monastic robes around the monument is a way of paying homage to the stupa.*

During the Sukhothai and Lanna periods the Thais built a great many stupas in northern Thailand. The earliest, erected at Chiang Mai, Chiang Rai, Chiang Saen, Lamphun and Lampang, featured large octagonal bases topped with slender superstructures probably influenced by Shan stupa architecture. Later stupas at Sukhothai, Si Satchanalai and Kamphaeng Phet mixed Khmer influences – such as the blunt, corncob-shaped *prang* – with native innovations such as lotus-bud finials.

A more powerful Thai kingdom called Ayuthaya developed in the Chao Phraya River basin to the south, and in 1376 Sukhothai was folded into the burgeoning Ayuthaya empire, along with Hanthawady or Pegu (Bago in today's Myanmar). After taking over former Khmer strongholds in U Thong and Lopburi, Ayuthaya's rulers annexed Angkor in 1451.

During its 417-year existence, the Ayuthaya empire became a crucible for all of the South-East Asian Buddhist cultures it came into contact with. Stupas multiplied at an even faster rate than at Sukhothai, and Ayuthaya's architects combined northern Thai, Shan, Burmese and especially Khmer motifs and techniques to produce the most elaborate stupas Thai culture has seen before or since. As at Bagan, the stupa-builders of Ayuthaya eventually expanded stupa bases into full-blown *prasada*, which they topped with semi-open relic chambers (*reuan thâat* in Thai). Next came a short, bell-shaped dome, followed by a lotus-bud spire inspired by Sukhothai stupas and topped with a short *plii*, akin in shape to the delicate banana flower.

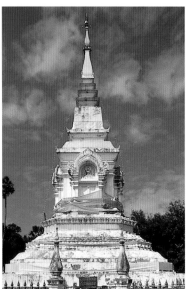

The Burmese invaded Ayuthaya in 1765 and after two years of warfare, left the capital in ruins. The Thais quickly re-cuperated and founded a new capital further south along the Chao Phraya River in 1769. Thailand's current royal lineage, the Chakri dynasty, dates to the founding of Bangkok in 1782, when Wat Phra Kaew, Wat Pho and several other royal-sponsored monasteries were constructed. Although this era in Thai art history is referred to as Ratanakosin (after the name of Bangkok's early royal district), stupa architecture followed late Ayuthaya models with only minor adaptations.

LEFT *In 1559 King Jayachettha of Chanthaburi (present-day Vientiane, Laos) extended his capital across the Mekong River and built this complex stupa, Phra That Bang Phuan, on the site of an earlier, as-yet-undated stupa. Near the provincial capital of Nong Khai, Thailand, the 34m monument combines the polygonal base of a Lao Lan Xang-style stupa with the middle section of a* prasat *(enclosed shrine) of Thailand's Ayuthaya period, a form itself influenced by early Khmer religious architecture. The four-sided, curvilinear spire at the top is typical of stupas throughout Laos and part of north-eastern Thailand.*

BELOW *A simple* dhyani *(meditation) Buddha sits in an arched niche at Phra That Bang Phuan. Local worshippers have added sacred cloth and an offering of fresh lotus buds.*

OPPOSITE *A gilded Ayuthaya-style stupa, constructed in the late 18th century, looms over surrounding temple buildings at Bangkok's Wat Phra Kaew (Wat Phra Si Ratana Satsadaram), the temple customarily used by Thai royalty since the founding of the capital.*

Once Thailand moved from an absolute to a constitutional monarchy in 1932, the royal coffers could no longer support the continuous construction of stupas and monasteries, which under their mostly self-supporting status tend to lack the degree of innovation seen in previous centuries. Dynastic upheavals, which no doubt contributed to artistic change, have also been noticeably absent since 1782.

LEFT *Rising to 127m, Nakhon Pathom's Phra Pathom Chedi is the tallest Buddhist monument in the world. The original stupa, buried within the massive glazed dome, was erected in the early 6th century, but in the early 11th century a Khmer king conquered the city and built a Brahman* prang *over it. The Burmese of Bagan sacked the city in 1057 and the* prang *lay in ruins until Thailand's King Mongkut had it encased in a new, larger stupa in 1860.*

BELOW LEFT *Phra That Phanom, the most revered Buddhist monument in north-eastern Thailand, follows the Lao model with its four-sided, undulating spire. The dating of the stupa is controversial, but some archaeologists set its age at about 1500 years. The spire of the 57m chedi is decorated with 110kg of gold.*

BELOW RIGHT *Women make offerings to two standing Buddha images in one of Phra Pathom Chedi's several adjacent shrines. The statues are gilded, one leaf at a time, by stupa visitors.*

OPPOSITE *Erected in the mid-13th century, the 78m chedi at Wat Phra Mahathat Woramahawihan in Nakhon Si Thammarat is crowned by a solid gold spire weighing several hundred kilograms. With its bell-shaped dome and prominent* harmika, *this stupa appears to have been influenced by classical Sri Lankan stupas.*

In the mid-14th century, Chao Fa Ngum, an exiled Lao warlord who enjoyed Khmer support, conquered Vientiane, Xieng Khuang, the Khorat Plateau (now part of north-eastern Thailand) and finally Chawa. This split the once-powerful Lanna empire into two: one side dominated by the northern Thai states and the other by Chao Fa Ngum's kingdom, called Lan Xang Hom Khao (Million Elephants and White Parasol).

LEFT *Schoolgirls from Savannakhet visit That Ing Hang, thought to have been built in the mid-16th century. This well-proportioned, 9m stupa is the second holiest in Laos after Pha That Luang. The base has been extended to three tiers, topped by a traditional Lao stupa and a gold umbrella weighing 450g. A hollow chamber in the lower section contains a collection of Buddha images. The French restored That Ing Hang in 1930, and although some original stucco decoration on the exterior remains intact, some of the sculpture in the outside niches is new.*

BELOW *That Chomsi, at the summit of a hill overlooking Luang Prabang, was originally erected in 1804 and restored in 1914. This stupa is the starting point for the colourful Lao New Year procession in mid-April.*

OPPOSITE *Pha That Phuan in the old capital of Xieng Khuang (today known as Muang Khun), is thought to date to the 16th century. Virtually every Buddhist monastery, shrine and stupa in Xieng Khuang was destroyed or seriously damaged during the Indochina War (1962–73).*

Little monumental Buddhist art was created during the Lan Xang era, but following Lan Xang's 15th-century break-up into three separate Lao city-states – Luang Prabang, Vientiane and Champasak – we begin to see a flourishing of Buddhist architecture. Although the presence of notable stupas in Laos is relatively minor compared to the number and quality one finds in Thailand and Myanmar, Lao stupa-builders did manage to forge a uniquely Lao style of stupa between the 15th and 18th centuries.

LEFT *At Wat That Luang in Luang Prabang, this large stupa was built to contain the ashes of King Sisavang Vong in 1910.*

BELOW *The slender Lao stupa near abandoned Wat Pah Huak in Luang Prabang resembles an elongated lotus bud and is reminiscent of some east Asian tower stupas.*

OPPOSITE *Pha That Pathum, more commonly known as That Makmo (Watermelon Stupa) because of its shape, stands on the grounds of the once royally sponsored Wat Wisunalat.*

Although not as highly venerated as the renowned Pha That Luang, perhaps the most unique stupa in Laos is the 34.5m Pha That Pathum (Lotus Stupa), on the grounds of Wat Wisunalat in Luang Prabang. Locally called That Makmo (Watermelon Stupa) because of its smooth, hemispherical shape, it was constructed in 1503 during the reign of King Wisunarat, and reconstructed in 1895 and 1932.

Other notable stupas in Laos, both of them following the four-sided, curvilinear lotus-bud style seen at Pha That Luang but with *prasada*-style bases, include Pha That Ing Hang near Savannakhet and Pha That Si Khotabong near Tha Khaek. Before the French colonisation of Laos, much of north-eastern Thailand came under Lao rule. Hence many classic Lao stupas – such as Phra That Phanom, famous for its vine-like decorations of gold – stand in Thailand, just across the Mekong River from Laos.

The most important stupa in today's Laos, Pha That Luang (Great Sacred Reliquary), symbolises both the Buddhist religion and Lao nationalism, and an image of the stupa appears on the national seal of the Lao People's Democratic Republic. Excavations at Pha That Luang suggest that a Mon or Khmer monastery might have stood here between the 11th and 13th centuries AD, and Vientiane's King Setthathirat chose this spot to begin construction of the great stupa in AD 1566. Following a Thai invasion in 1828, Pha That Luang was abandoned until it was restored under French rule in the early 20th century.

Walkways around three diminishing terraces, with stairways between, are meant to be mounted by the faithful. As at Borobudur, each level of the monument has different architectural features in which Buddhist doctrine is encoded, and visitors are invited to contemplate the meaning of these features as they circumambulate.

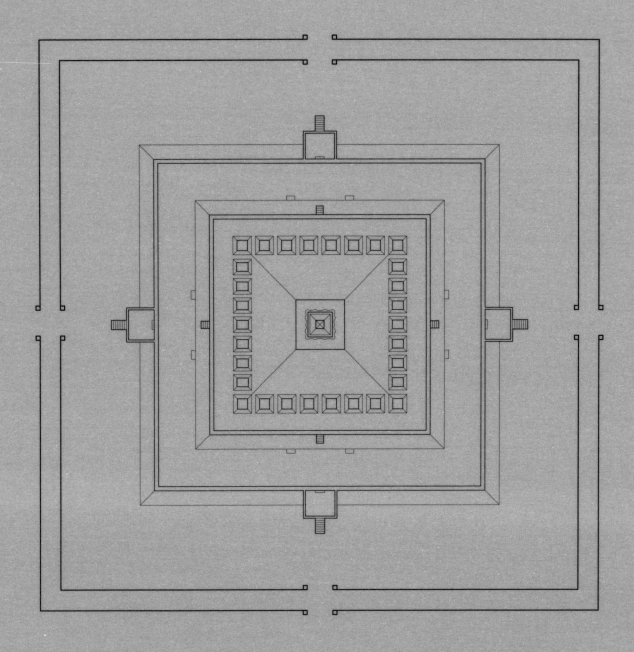

The square mandala represents expansion to the four corners of the earth.
On the stupa's second level 30 small stupas symbolise the 30 Buddhist
perfections, beginning with alms-giving and ending with equanimity.
The lotus-bud shaped spire is said to symbolise the growth of a lotus
from the seed in a muddy lake bottom to a bloom over the lake's surface,
a metaphor for human advancement from ignorance to enlightenment.

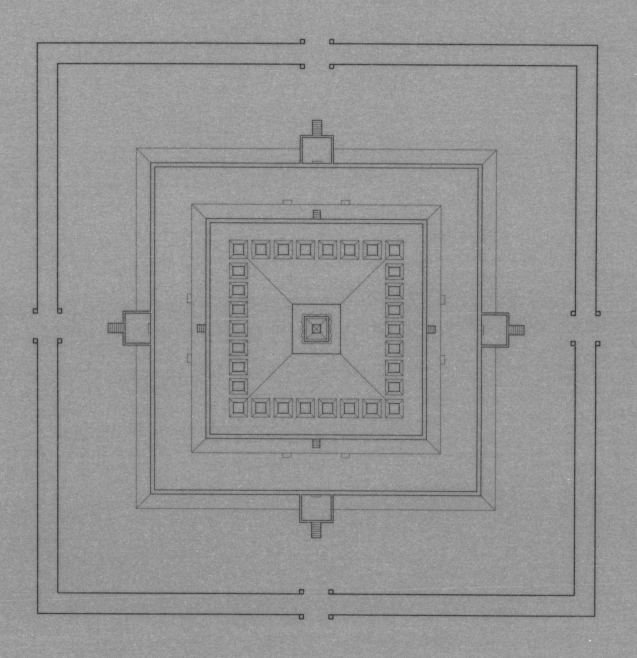

The square mandala represents expansion to the four corners of the earth.
On the stupa's second level 30 small stupas symbolise the 30 Buddhist
perfections, beginning with alms-giving and ending with equanimity.
The lotus-bud shaped spire is said to symbolise the growth of a lotus
from the seed in a muddy lake bottom to a bloom over the lake's surface,
a metaphor for human advancement from ignorance to enlightenment.

KATHMANDU VALLEY CHAITYAS

Although Buddhist art in the Kathmandu Valley can be traced to the Licchavi era (3rd to 9th centuries AD), most of what can be seen today dates no further back than the mid-16th century, when a major cultural renaissance swept through the valley. Even at that time Buddhism was a minority religion in central Nepal, and it remains so today. Mixed with animism and shamanism, as well as Hinduism, the religion persists among the Newars of the Kathmandu Valley and may well be the only surviving thread of Indian Mahayana Buddhism.

Over the last 500 years, Newari Buddhists have adorned Kathmandu Valley with roughly 2000 stupas, one of the largest concentrations found anywhere in the world (only Myanmar's Bagan boasts a greater number). The Sanskrit *chaitya* is the preferred term for stupa in Buddhist Nepal, although the Newars commonly use the colloquial *chibha* as well. Style and scope vary widely from small, vertical Licchavi *chaityas* to the grand mandala-plan Svayambhunath and Bodhnath.

One of the major iconographical differences between the stupas of Kathmandu Valley and most of those in India, Sri Lanka and mainland South-East Asia is the sculptural presence of the five Jina (Victorious) Buddhas. Each of these is associated with a different cardinal direction, *mudra* (hand position) and corresponding set of religious attributes. Unlike the 'historical' Buddhas who are born into the world as human teachers, the Jina Buddhas represent cosmic principles of the *buddhadharma* (Buddha's teaching) visible only to the adept.

Four of the Jina Buddha sculptures are oriented to the four cardinal directions. Since a stupa's solid centre can't be viewed from the outside, Vairochana, the Great Illuminator, may be displayed in the south-east or, less commonly, the north-east corner of smaller stupas. On the larger, monumental stupas patterned after Svayambhunath and Bodhnath, Vairochana is often represented by large, almond-shaped eyes painted onto the cuboid *harmika* which separates dome and spire.

Further appearances by Mahayana and Tantric religious figures may include Bodhisattvas or Buddhas-to-be, who are easily distinguishable from Buddhas by their crowns, bracelets or other royal adornments. Key Bodhisattvas found on Kathmandu Valley stupas include Avalokiteshvara (carrying a lotus flower), Manjushri (accompanied by a book and a sword) and Maitreya (accompanied by a small stupa, a vase and a flower). Stupas with more complex ornamentation may also display sculptures or relief carvings of Prajñas (female consorts) for the five Jina Buddhas. The latter occupy intermediate compass points on a separate level of the stupa and include Pandura (south-west), Shyama Tara (north-west), Lochana (north-east), Mamaki (south-east) and Prajñaparamita (also known as Vajradhatisvari, either east-south-east or east-north-east).

Each of the Buddhas, Bodhisattvas and Prajñas is associated with a specific colour, and archaeological evidence suggests stupa carvings may once have been painted accordingly. The positioning of this assortment of Buddhas and Bodhisattvas, along with a stupa's general plan, often creates the Vajradhatu (Diamond Element) mandala of Vajrayana Buddhism. The mandala effect is enhanced by receding corners in a stupa's square plinth, producing a 20-cornered pattern known as *vimshatikona*, a basic shape for many Vajrayana mandalas.

KATHMANDU VALLEY CHAITYAS

THE FIVE JINA BUDDHAS	DIRECTION	COLOUR	MUDRA
AMOGHASIDDHI *UNFAILING SUCCESS*	NORTH	GREEN	ABHAYA *PROTECTION*
AMITABHA *BOUNDLESS LIGHT*	WEST	RED	DHYANA *MEDITATION*
RATNASAMBHAVA *JEWEL-BORN*	SOUTH	YELLOW	VARADA *WISH-GRANTING*
AKSHOBHYA *IMMOVABLE*	EAST	BLUE	BHUMISPARSA *EARTH-TOUCHING*
VAIROCHANA *ILLUMINATOR*	CENTRE	WHITE	DHARMACHAKRA *TURNING OF THE WHEEL OF DHARMA*

The Licchavi *chaitya* – so called because the style is supposed to have originated during the valley's Licchavi dynastic period, although some monuments may have been built much later – reduces the scale of the classic stupa to its most intimate level. Often standing only waist high (the largest, at Chabahil, measures 180cm), the typical Licchavi *chaitya* is constructed of stone blocks carved and assembled to shape the base, dome, *harmika* (commonly called the *gala* or 'neck' in Kathmandu) and spire. Stupa architecture at the north Indian Buddhist centres of Rajgir and Nalanda influenced the Licchavi *chaitya* plan, although local innovation produced distinctively native interpretations.

ABOVE *The Licchavi* chaitya *at the Rudravarna Mahavihar temple in Patan is of the* caturvyuha *or 'four manifestations' variety, with Buddha images on all four sides. Local Buddhists have left offerings of flowers and paper umbrellas.*

LEFT *Red and yellow votive powder is often placed on the heads of Buddha reliefs as a sign of veneration. This Licchavi* chaitya *at Tham Bahal has obviously been moved, since its original base is missing.*

BOTTOM *This unique Licchavi stupa features a* padmavali *or lotus-leaf base. The stupa is covered with red votive powder and flower offerings.*

OPPOSITE *The empty niches of this Licchavi-style chaitya in Kathmandu would once have been filled, on certain religious occasions, with metal inserts depicting various Buddhas, Bodhisattvas and Prajñas. As with many votive stupas in the Kathmandu Valley, the finial and base are missing.*

LICCHAVI CHAITYAS

Skilled Newari artisans carved the stone faces of the miniature stupas to create rich figurative ornamentation, including floral motifs, Buddha and Bodhisattva figures and niches to contain them. Those Licchavi *chaityas* whose arched niches today stand empty were probably intended to contain repoussé metal figures which could be affixed to the stupas during festival events and easily removed afterwards.

ABOVE *A well-executed relief of Avalokiteshvara – identifiable by the small Buddha figure in the headdress – stands in a stupa niche along with two disciples.*

LEFT *This highly ornate Licchavi-style stupa contains all the classic features, including carvings of the Jina Buddhas and associated deities. The base consists of a* yoni, *a womb-shaped symbol linked with the Hindu cult of Shakti.*

BOTTOM *The stupa in a courtyard of Oku Bahal in Patan stands on its original base. The elaborate finial decorated with* nagas *(serpent deities) may have been added later, like the floral trellis.*

OPPOSITE *The Chabahil Mahachaitya, one of the oldest in the Kathmandu Valley, is thought to have been the first to depart from classical Ashokan models, and may itself have served as a partial model for the Bodhnath Mahachaitya and later Nepali stupas. Legend ascribes the stupa to King Ashoka's daughter Charumati in the 3rd century BC, though all evidence suggests construction between the 5th and 7th centuries AD. Note the smaller Licchavi-style stupa in the foreground.*

Around 260 Licchavi *chaityas* or fragments thereof can be seen in the valley today. Most are reconstructions – often fragments combined with newer elements, particularly high, multitiered bases – and virtually all have been moved from their original locations. Many Licchavi *chaityas* can be found standing in the courtyards of Newari Buddhist temples or in sunken neighbourhood fountains. Devotees make frequent offerings of flowers and apply brilliant red and yellow votive powder to surviving Jina Buddha or Bodhisattva figures.

Four large earthen mounds stand at near-cardinal points surrounding the ancient Newari city of Patan at the southern extent of the Kathmandu Valley. The wide, relatively shallow hemispheric forms easily lend themselves to comparison with Ashokan stupas in northern India, Pakistan and Afghanistan. Indeed, Nepali tradition claims King Ashoka paid a visit to the valley and ordered the construction of the stupas in the 3rd century BC. A less romantic but equally popular notion has it that the mounds were erected when Patan was founded in the 4th century AD, but epigraphic evidence has yet to provide any confirmation.

LEFT *A so-called Ashokan stupa at the northern edge of Patan, with a Nepali-style* harmika *and* chattravali, *is flanked by two more standard Newari stupas. The original mound is thought to have been covered with turf.*

OPPOSITE *Patan's eastern Ashoka stupa probably remains closer to its original form, minus the* harmika *and retaining wall.*

PATAN'S 'ASHOKAN' STUPAS

Local artisans added finials and low retaining walls to all four mounds in the late 19th and early 20th centuries, and decorated the walls with Jina Buddhas and other Vajrayana icons. While the northern stupa has been covered with brick and plaster, the other three display the original exposed turf. The northern monument also bears an elaborate superstructure, consisting of a *harmika* and a 13-level finial obviously inspired by the Bodhnath Mahachaitya. The southern mound, largest of the four at 47.4m in diameter and 11.8m in height, is mounted by a hemispherical finial resembling a smaller stupa. Despite the modifications, all four Patan stupas have retained an atmosphere of rustic devotion.

Towering above the city's brick and cement skyline, the 'great stupas' or *mahachaityas* of the Kathmandu Valley are objects of intense veneration for Nepali and Tibetan Buddhists, and of great interest to the thousands of tourists who visit Kathmandu each year.

According to Nepali mythology, the Kathmandu Valley once formed the bottom of a vast, deep lake inhabited only by *nagas* (serpent gods). Vipaswi Buddha – the first Buddha to have been born in the human realm – visited the lake during the Satya Yuga, or Truth Age, and sowed a lotus seed that blossomed into a thousand-petalled lotus floating in the centre. On each of the lotus petals sat a Bodhisattva, and in the centre of the lotus, Svayambhu (Self-Born), a form of the Adi or Primordial Buddha, projected a dazzling light.

LEFT Svayambhunath Mahachaitya at dusk.

CENTRE The gold-plated harmika on Svayambhunath Mahachaitya is painted with the eyes of Vairochana Buddha, as is customary for Nepali mahachaityas.

OPPOSITE The morning mist surrounds Svayambhunath Hill like the primordial lake that Nepali legend claims once enveloped the spot. Meanwhile, the sun appears like the self-born lotus light that issued from the hilltop when Manjushri cut off its tip with his great sword.

THE MAHACHAITYAS *Svayambhunath*

In a later era the Bodhisattva Manjushri visited the sacred lake and, using his flaming sword of wisdom, cut four gorges in the surrounding mountains to drain the valley so that humans could more easily worship the light-filled Svayambhu lotus. To support the waterless flower, Manjushri built a mountain around the stem, and an Indian king-turned-ascetic later capped the shining flower with a stupa to protect the light from the coming of the present age, Kali Yuga. Thus, according to legend, was born Svayambhunath, the 'protector of Svayambhu'.

Mythology aside, Svayambhunath stands to the west of Kathmandu and is thought to be the oldest *chaitya* site in Kathmandu Valley, perhaps dating to the 5th-century reign of King Vrishadeva. However the stupa might have originally appeared, it took on its present shape during a major 15th-century restoration. The stupa's 22m wooden axis pole (called *yahsi* in Nepali), a component of virtually all *mahachaityas*, has been replaced several times over the centuries, most recently in 1918.

ABOVE *Two Licchavi-style stupas stand in a courtyard adjacent to Svayambhunath Mahachaitya.*

LEFT *A* vajracharya *or Newari Buddhist lay priest performs an elaborate* puja *(religious ritual with a specific purpose) at Svayambhunath.*

FAR LEFT *Svayambhunath Hill is studded with smaller stupas, including these two roughly modelled after Svayambhunath itself, and the diminutive Licchavi-style stupa in the right foreground.*

BOTTOM *At the Kagyüpa monastery adjacent to Svayambhunath, Situ Rinpoche performs a rare 'red hat' ceremony.*

OPPOSITE *As part of a wedding procession, a brass band circumambulates Svayambhunath, passing in front of one of the Indian-style* shikharas *that flank the* mahachaitya.

During festivals celebrated at Svayambhunath, tens of thousands of worshippers stream up the hill on which the *mahachaitya* stands, and then walk clockwise around the stupa to gain religious merit through *pradakshina* (circumambulation). On such occasions, stupa trustees douse the whitewashed dome with a mixture of mustard oil and turmeric, leaving behind a deep yellow stain in a rough lotus-petal pattern.

Thought to be only slightly more recent than Svayambhunath, the *mahachaitya* of Bodhnath (the Enlightenment Protector), north-east of Kathmandu, has long been an important place of pilgrimage for Tibetan Buddhists. King Manadeva I constructed Bodhnath towards the end of the 5th century, although the stupa probably took on its current basic form when a Tibetan lama encased the original dome with a new one in the 16th century. Although the dome is shallower and broader, the similarity of the stupa's cuboid *harmika* and 13-tiered spire (symbolising the 13 *bhumi*, or stages of Bodhisattva-hood) to those at Svayambhunath suggests that the latter was employed as a prototype. However, while Svayambhunath stands on a circular plinth, Bodhnath features a more complex 20-cornered *vimshatikona*-shaped plinth. Together with the icons found along the stupa's perimeters, this design unfolds into the Dharmadhatu (Dharma Element) mandala. Bodhnath is nearly twice the height of Svayambhunath.

Considered particularly sacred among Tibetan pilgrims, Bodhnath – or 'Boudha' as it is commonly called in Kathmandu – is said to contain relics of Kashyapa Buddha, the third Buddha of this era. Day and night, a steady flow of worshippers circles the stupa with intense devotion, turning metal prayer wheels lined up along the base, then climbing the triple plinth to offer prayers, mantras and prostrations. Since the 1959 exodus of Tibetan refugees to the Kathmandu Valley, the district around Bodhnath has filled with Tibetan Buddhist monasteries, Tibetan carpet factories and handicrafts dealers.

Bodhnath

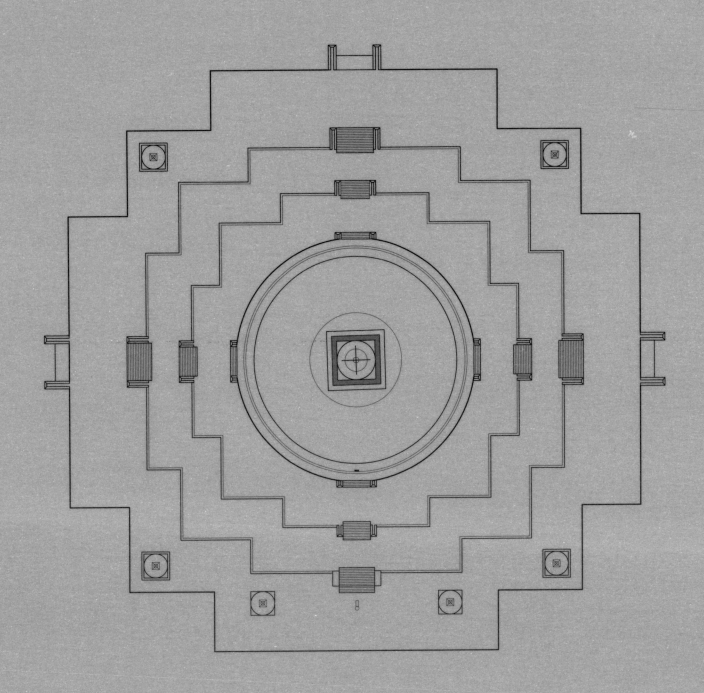

A classic Nepali dome, reliquary box and spire top three diminishing *vimshatikona* bases, together forming the Dharmadhatu (Dharma Element) mandala.

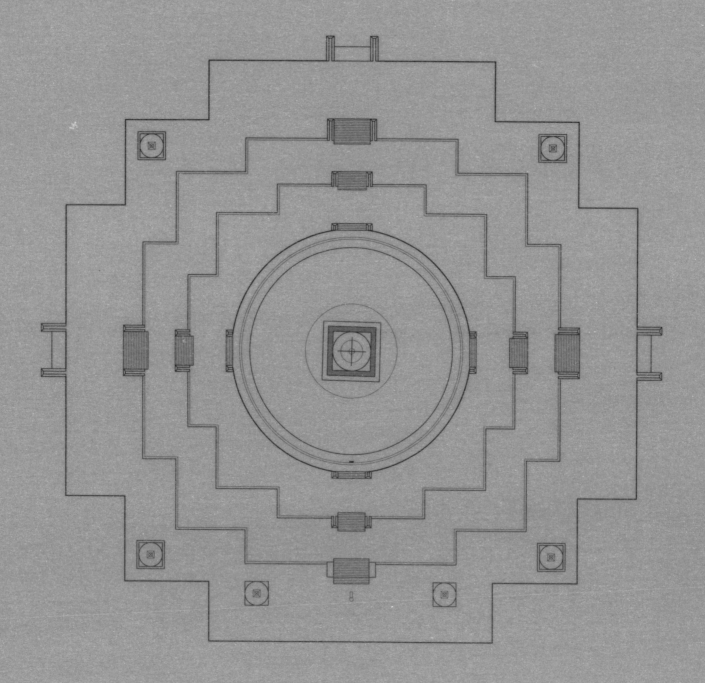

A classic Nepali dome, reliquary
box and spire top three diminishing
vimshatikona bases, together
forming the Dharmadhatu
(Dharma Element) mandala.

A STUPA CROSSES CULTURES

Chorten Tongdrol Chenmo (Tibetan for 'the great stupa that liberates upon seeing'), recently built near the southern edge of Kathmandu Valley, mirrors the eclecticism of Buddhism in today's world: it is a copy of an ancient Burmese stupa; it was built by Newari craftsmen from Nepal; and the rituals and ceremonies of its construction and consecration hail from the Tibetan Buddhist tradition. Although renovation of ancient stupas is a common practice all over the Buddhist world, the construction of new stupas is relatively rare. Chorten Tongdrol Chenmo thus serves as a contemporary example of the motivations and methods by which such an auspicious project is carried out.

The brick foundation for the Chorten Tongdrol Chenmo is laid in Godavari, Nepal.

Newari and Tibetan volunteers apply silver-toned paint to fired-clay tsha-tsha. *Later, a total of 100,000 votives were interred in the stupa.*

A kalasha, *or ritual vase, filled with sacred objects, including written Tibetan mantras,* ringsel *(relics of venerated Tibetan Bodhisattvas or gurus), Buddha relics and 'dharma pills' made of sacred earthen compounds and herbs. Five such vases were interred in the base of the stupa.*

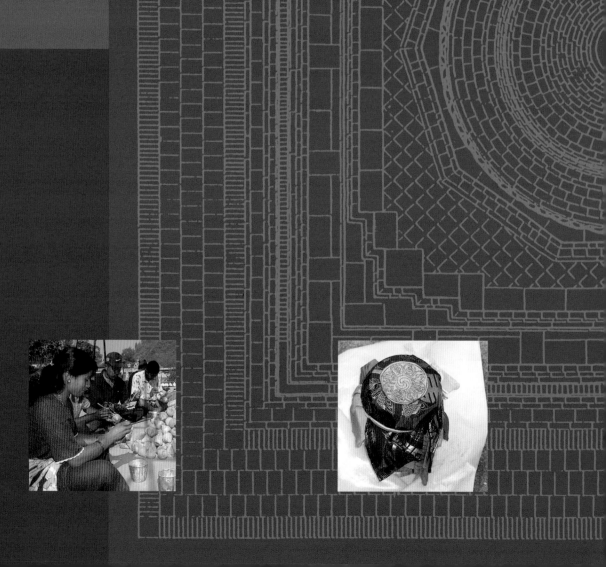

When Tulku Urgyen Rinpoche, a renowned Tibetan meditation master, died in 1996, a long-time American student of his sponsored the renovation of a collapsing Bagan-era stupa in Myanmar to honour his teacher. When the student later showed photographs of the stupa to Chatral Sang-Gye Dorje Rinpoche, a great Nyingma master living in Nepal, Rinpoche suggested building such a stupa in the Kathmandu Valley. Another student of Tulku Urgyen Rinpoche, Yvonne Wong, agreed to sponsor the project.

Detailed drawings, measurements and photos of the original stupa were acquired from Myanmar. Niels Gutschow, a German architect and architectural historian living in Nepal, agreed to supervise the construction, and proposed that rather than importing Burmese masons, his trained team of Newari masons could build the stupa.

One of the five kalasha *after its placement in the stupa base, topped with a prayer scarf and flower petals*

Tsha-tsha — small, stupa-shaped votives filled with tiny prayer scrolls — are inserted into the foundation of the stupa.

A Burmese monk and a Tibetan monk offer prayers while placing sacred objects into the base of the stupa.

The base and dome completed, workers lift the juniper tsok-shing *(life-tree or centre pole) so that it can be inserted into the middle of the dome.*

Installing the stupa finial.

Chatral Sang-Gye Dorje Rinpoche (white beard, seated) conducts a series of rituals to consecrate the new stupa.

A woman touches her forehead to the prayer-scarf-festooned new stupa.

Lamas conduct consecration rituals for the stupa.

The village of Godavari, perched in a small mountain valley rich in medicinal herbs and considered by local Vajrayana Buddhists to be one of 24 particularly sacred locations, was chosen as the site. Eight Tibetan nuns commenced the making of 100,000 *tsha-tsha*: small votive images made of clay and filled with Tibetan prayer scrolls. In February 1999, Chatral Rinpoche performed the *sa blang* (earth-taking ritual), requesting permission from the earth deities and local spirits to construct the stupa. In March, the foundation was dug and the five *kalasha* (auspicious vases symbolising prosperity) were placed in the foundation. The vast number of *tsha-tsha* were placed in the chamber of the base of the stupa during April and May.

Bijay Basukala, the Newari engineer in charge of construction, found that the making of the bricks was the project's biggest technical challenge, since the lotus base and the eleven upper rings all required hand-carved bricks larger than any previously produced in Nepal. Nearly half of each firing showed cracks or other imperfections, so the work had to be done repeatedly to achieve a sufficient number.

In August, monks prepared the 4.9m, solid juniper *tsok-shing* ('life-tree' or centre pole) by painting the wood red and writing auspicious texts in gold, wrapping the pole in paper strips inscribed with sacred texts, wrapping the whole in silk, and finally encasing it in copper to preserve it. In September, the installation of the *tsok-shing* took place with appropriate ritual. In October, the *gajur* (crowning jewel ornament), which Newari craftsmen fire-gilded using 180g of gold, was carried up the bamboo scaffolding and set atop the rings while Chatral Rinpoche and his monks intoned chants and prayers.

Four thousand people, including religious masters from the Burmese, Tibetan and Newari traditions, attended the three-day *rab gnas* (final consecration ceremony) from 30 October to 1 November 1999. The invitation to the consecration read, in part, 'This stupa will benefit beings by naturally causing them to abide by the 10 virtuous actions, to gather the accumulations, to purify obscuration and eventually to attain the level of unbiased nirvana'.

By Pam Ross

Pam Ross is the former coordinator of the University of Wisconsin Nepal Student Program. She has lived in Nepal for many years.

The final consecration of the Chorten Tongdrol Chenmo.

Illustrations of Chorten Tongdrol Chenmo are by Niels Gutschow and Bijay Basukala.

INTO THE HIMALAYAS

OPPOSITE *Many stupas in the Nepal Himalayas show a mixture of Tibetan and Nepali influences. In the case of this stupa at Helambhu in central Nepal, the dome is Tibetan in appearance, the spire Nepali, while the overall design may derive from Bön shrines pre-dating both Himalayan Buddhism and Newari Buddhism.*

As Buddhism made its ascent from the plains of north-eastern India to the Himalayan mountain ranges of Nepal and Tibet during the 6th and 7th centuries AD, the inhabitants of these areas adapted the religion to suit their temperament and cultural background. Buddhist doctrine also began to draw from India's all-encompassing Hindu traditions, particularly from Tantric literature and practices, which emphasise specific liturgies to achieve specific spiritual results. Around this same time, the Himalayan kingdoms came into contact with the Buddhist schools of China, Nepal and Central Asia, each of which offered its own unique twists on *buddhadharma*.

Once it reached the Tibetan Plateau, Buddhism also had to contend with Bön, an indigenous mix of shamanism and animism whose priests enjoyed broad power over much of the region. Seeking to establish a cogent line of Buddhist teachings, Tibetan king Trisong Detsen (AD 790–858) invited several Buddhist gurus from the Indian subcontinent to found Samye Monastery in southern Tibet. The most famous of these teachers, a Tantric adept named Padmasambhava, hailed from Pakistan's Swat Valley and is credited with the subjugation of the Tibetan demons who gave the Bön priests their power. For this achievement he earned the title Guru Rinpoche, 'Precious Teacher'. Tibetans today regard Guru Rinpoche as the second Buddha of the current era.

By the mid-9th century, the fragile Buddhist lineage in Tibet had collapsed as Bön regained power and religious persecution drove Buddhism underground. Meanwhile, yet another wave of Buddhism, based in Bengal, emerged under the Pala and Sena dynasties (AD 730–1197). This Bengali school of Buddhism, a permutation of Mahayana doctrine known as Vajrayana (Diamond Vehicle), held much influence at India's greatest Buddhist centre of learning, Nalanda University in Bihar.

Nalanda proved to be an essential link in a Buddhist web that ultimately connected Tibet, India and the Sailendra-Srivijaya kingdoms of Sumatra and Java. Among the most influential Buddhist scholars at Nalanda was Bengal-born Srigana Dipankara (AD 982–1055), who followed the teachings of his Sumatran guru, Dharmakirti. Better known today by the honorific title Atisha, 'The Incomparable One', Dipankara made an arduous journey to western Tibet in 1040 at the invitation of the Guge kingdom. Although he originally planned to stay only three years, Atisha Dipankara never left Tibet and eventually died at Nathang Monastery near Lhasa in 1055.

Although well versed in the tantras, Atisha stressed monastic discipline and the gradual approach to enlightenment, a perspective that differed from both the earlier esoteric Buddhism in Tibet under Guru Rinpoche and the 'sudden enlightenment' introduced from Tang dynasty China. Atisha's Tibetan disciples founded the Kadampa monastic sect, which eventually developed into today's Gelugpa school, the most conservative Tibetan sect (requiring lifelong monastic celibacy, for example) and the one to which the 14th Dalai Lama belongs.

From the 11th century onwards, the Himalayas became a crucible for all these outside Buddhist influences from northern India, from China and from Sumatra-Java – as well as surviving Bön tenets – to produce Lamaism. Like the earlier Vajrayana of Bengal and South-East Asia, Lamaism possesses strong Tantric elements, while adding the hereditary system of reincarnated living Bodhisattvas and Buddhas unique to the Himalayan lands and Mongolia. Along with providing an obvious way for property to be inherited by the Buddhist clergy, the lama system created a complex clerical hierarchy somewhat analogous to that of the Roman Catholic Church in the West.

Lamaism's Tantric legacy invests much spiritual power in certain inanimate objects, such as the *dorje* (hand-held thunderbolt symbol), *gau* (deity amulet worn around the neck), *tsha-tsha* (votive tablets), *dadar* (arrow symbol used in rites of fertility and longevity) and, of course, the stupa.

RIGHT *A very plain whitewashed stupa, save for its gold finial, at Labrang Monastery in Xiahe, Gansu Province, China.*

BELOW *A Buddhist nun walks among greying prayer flags and stupas at Lhagang Monastery in Dardo County, Kham (Sichuan Province, China). This single site contains 124 stupas, one of which has been seen to vibrate spontaneously.*

OPPOSITE *With a lopsided stupa in the background, lamas and monks lead a procession in a high mountain valley in Nubri, north-central Nepal.*

THE CHORTEN

The Tibetan translation for 'stupa', *chorten*, may have been applied to Bön monuments of similar function prior to the stupa's first appearance in the Himalayan region in the 9th century. In keeping with the pre-Buddhist Bön and Tantric emphasis on linking spirit with the inanimate world, Lamaism views the Buddhist stupa as substantially more than a tribute to the pantheon of Buddhas and Bodhisattvas, a reminder of their teachings or a designated place of worship. While stupas in all Buddhist traditions carry a symbolic message through their overall design and iconography, and provide a medium for the making of religious merit, the follower of Tibetan Buddhism takes the vehicle one step further.

For the Himalayan Buddhist, the stupa represents a living embodiment of *dharmakaya*, the 'body of the doctrine'. Rather than seeing the stupa as a mere memorial or a symbolic teaching vehicle, the Himalayan believer invests the stupa with the capacity to spur the observer towards nirvana simply by seeing or contemplating it.

The Buddha said that whoever sees a dharmakaya stupa will be liberated by the sight of it. The breeze near the stupa liberates by its touch, and the tinkling of the small bells hanging on the stupa liberates by its sound. Having thus experienced this stupa, by thinking of one's experience of it, one is liberated through recollection.

Dilgo Khyentse Rinpoche

In order to provide this extraordinary function, however, the Himalayan stupa must be carefully constructed to yield correct proportions, and all steps of the construction and consecration must be supported by correct ritual. By this careful adherence to external parameters the stupa becomes a Tantric object. Stupas of this kind (often called Tibetan stupas) can be found today wherever Lamaism has taken hold, that is to say Tibet, Bhutan, Mongolia, western China and the mountainous areas of northern Nepal and northern India.

RIGHT *Samye Monastery, Tibet's oldest, began construction in the 9th century and assumed a mandala-like shape.*

BELOW *This ruined stupa is said to contain the relics of the 8th-century Sanskrit-Tibetan translator Chokrolui Gyeltsen. The stupa stands at the edge of Mt Hepori, one of the four sacred hills of Tibet. The Tsangpo River, Tibet's lifeline, can be seen in the background.*

BOTTOM *Horseback racing at a festival in Lo village, Nubri, Nepal.*

OPPOSITE *A stupa assembled of roughly carved stones at Mt Kailash, the most sacred mountain peak in the Himalayas.*

Although Himalayan stupas share the same three main elements – base, dome and superstructure – as stupas found elsewhere in Asia, the patterns followed are much more formalised and less innovative than those of the Indian subcontinent and South-East Asia. There may have been a transition phase between the stupa types of northern India and those of the Himalayas, but if so no surviving examples have yet been found.

Plans, shapes and proportions have remained relatively standard since the early 14th century. Although Tibetan Buddhists have justified this standardisation with 'lost' Sanskrit texts translated into Tibetan, the Himalayan stupa has no counterpart in India and the style seems to have originated on the Tibetan Plateau. In minute detail, the Tibetan texts lay out the proper methods for site selection, construction and consecration of stupas. Along with architectural methods and materials, these texts also stipulate formulae for mantras, *mudras* and occult substances associated with stupa creation.

The classic design features a standard 'lion plinth' – a tall, box-like base – topped by four receding terraces which may be square or circular in shape depending on which of the eight allowed variations has been chosen (see page 128). Atop the last terrace stands an *anda* in the shape of an inverted alms bowl, perhaps the single most immediately identifiable feature of the Himalayan stupa. Often referred to in Tibetan commentaries as a 'vase' (*kumbha* in Sanskrit) rather than a 'dome', this section increases in diameter as it ascends, creating the exact opposite line of virtually all other stupa domes in the Buddhist world.

ABOVE *With four square tiers and a Buddha niche in the dome, a stupa of the type known as Shravasti, commemorating miracles performed by the Buddha, stands in front of Gomar Monastery in Amdo (Qinghai Province, China).*

BELOW *This stupa at Langmusa Monastery, Amdo, resembles the Tibetan kumbums (see page 142–5), and may be modelled after the 'auspicious doorways' type. However, in this case the monastic cells themselves are found in the base.*

OPPOSITE *In Mewa, far-eastern Amdo, stands a stupa of the 'auspicious doorways' type, associated with the Buddha's first discourse in Sarnath.*

Above the *anda*, the *harmika* of the Himalayan stupa has been reduced to a very short and relatively narrow section. This in turn is mounted by a long finial which, as on many late Nepali stupas, consists mainly of 13 diminishing rings. Rather than relate the rings to the 13 stages of Bodhisattva-hood, the Tibetan texts state that they represent the 10 powers (*dashabala*) of the Buddha, plus the three foundations of mindfulness peculiar to Buddhas.

Crowning the rings are an upturned crescent moon supporting a spherical sun – symbolising the coming together of compassion and wisdom, the Tantric feminine and masculine – topped by a smaller sphere standing for the union of these pairs, which is *bodhichitra* or enlightenment. A flat, round element between the rings and the spheres represents the original stupa umbrella, a sign of royal protection and sponsorship.

BELOW *Painted around 1630, this unusually brilliant mural at Lhakang Marpo in Tsaparang, western Tibet, catalogues the eight Himalayan stupa types.*

BOTTOM *Although at first glance these stupas at Jiuzhaigou in Kham appear to be the classic eight Himalayan Buddhist archetypes, the reverse swastikas suggest they belong to the pre-Buddhist Bön religion.*

OPPOSITE *Near Dzogchen Monastery in Kham (now part of Sichuan Province, China), monks rest beside a row of the eight Himalayan stupa types.*

Variations that do occur in Himalayan stupas follow the Tibetan belief that the Buddha mandated the construction of eight types of stupa, corresponding to the eight great events of his life and their associated pilgrimage spots. The principal differences among the eight types concern the stepped terraces between the lion plinth and the vase. Although almost always numbering four (occasionally three or five), the terraces may be circular, square-cornered, octagonal or even 20-cornered.

Tibetan texts agree as to the basic designs these eight stupa types should follow, but the various texts offer roughly 10 different explanations of what the eight represent.

Although the eight Himalayan stupas occasionally appear side by side in one line or in two rows of four, most commonly they stand alone. In Himalayan lands today, the most commonly seen lone stupa of the eight types – the *mahabodhi*, or enlightenment stupa – displays a plain, four-tiered base and a simple dome with no Buddha niches. Devotees typically whitewash the entire monument from base to spire.

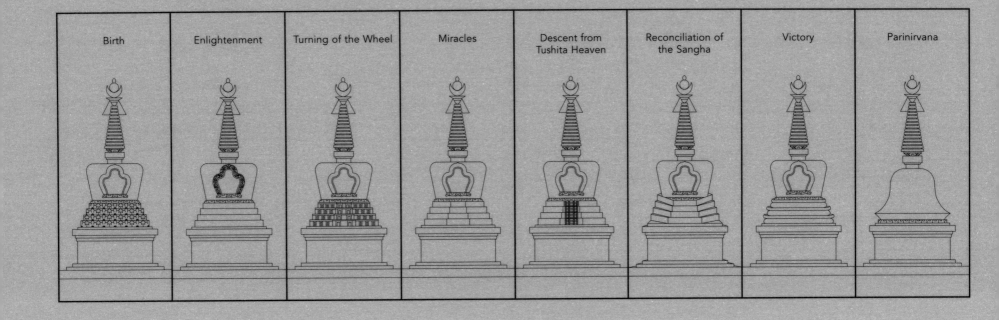

| Birth | Enlightenment | Turning of the Wheel | Miracles | Descent from Tushita Heaven | Reconciliation of the Sangha | Victory | Parinirvana |

THE MOST CITED VERSION OF THE EIGHT HIMALAYAN STUPA TYPES

EVENT	PLACE	DESIGN
BIRTH	LUMBINI	ROUND TIERS DECORATED WITH LOTUS PETALS; ONE LARGE BUDDHA NICHE ON THE DOME
ENLIGHTENMENT	BODHGAYA	PLAIN SQUARE TIERS; NO BUDDHA NICHE
TURNING OF THE WHEEL	SARNATH	SQUARE TIERS WITH AUSPICIOUS DOORWAYS (NICHES) ALONG EACH LEVEL AND EACH SIDE OF THE BASE
MIRACLES	SHRAVASTI	PLAIN SQUARE TIERS; ONE BUDDHA NICHE ON EACH SIDE OF THE DOME
DESCENT FROM TUSHITA HEAVEN	SANKASHYA	SAME AS MIRACLES, ADDING A SET OF STAIRS LEADING FROM EACH NICHE
RECONCILIATION OF THE SANGHA	RAJGIR	SQUARE (OR OCCASIONALLY OCTAGONAL) TIERS DECORATED WITH FLOWERS
VICTORY	VAISHALI	ROUND TIERS DECORATED WITH DHARMACHAKRA (DHARMA WHEELS)
PARINIRVANA	KUSHINAGAR	NO TIERS; NO BUDDHA NICHE; DOME IS OFTEN BELL-SHAPED RATHER THAN VASE-SHAPED

ABOVE *A stupa perches on a corner of the walls around remote Thöling Monastery in far-western Tibet, built around 1014–25. The architecture at Thöling is characteristic of the ancient Guge kingdom, and arguably far-west Tibet's highest artistic achievement. The great Indian Buddhist scholar Atisha resided at this monastery from 1042 to 1045.*

RIGHT *Tabo Gompa is one of the most important monasteries in the Tibetan Buddhist world, and probably where the current Dalai Lama will retire. It is located in Spiti, India, which in the 11th century was part of the Tibetan Guge kingdom.*

BELOW *The tiered, stepped base and flared dome at this stupa at Thöling Monastery lend an almost Burmese flavour to the monument, not by coincidence, since both Tibetan and Burmese Buddhist architects were influenced by the Pala/Sena art of Bengal.*

OPPOSITE *Himalayan Buddhists consider these reddish rock formations at Tirthapuri, an area of geysers and hot springs near Mt Kailash, to be 'self-born' stupas. So highly revered are these formations that, after Mt Kailash and Lake Manasarovar, this is the holiest pilgrimage site in western Tibet.*

ABOVE *Stone-block stupas dusted with snow echo the shape and colour of the surrounding peaks, including 6812m Ama Dablam.*

RIGHT *Covered with budding vegetation, this Nepali stupa at Takshindu Pass in northern Nepal's Sherpa country might appear to be abandoned if it weren't for the relatively new finial.*

BELOW *Although in the Khumbu region of Himalayan Nepal, with its hemispherical dome and square-tiered spire this stupa is more Newari than Himalayan in style. The pile of rocks in the foreground is a cairn, placed there by Tibetan travellers to mark a mountain pass.*

OPPOSITE *At Tangboche (Tengpoche) Monastery in Khumbu, a blizzard blurs the outlines of a classic Himalayan stupa as a line of trekkers files by in search of shelter.*

BELOW LEFT *Inside a gateway stupa in Nepal's remote Dolpo region, the ceiling is adorned with nine esoteric — possibly Bön — mandalas and the walls are covered with Jina Buddhas, Bodhisattvas and Prajñas.*

BOTTOM *Dolpo's rustic stupas are assembled of air-dried mud bricks to produce two or three block-like tiers. Occasionally a simple porch is built on an upper tier to provide shelter.*

OPPOSITE *An isolated gateway stupa in Tarap, Dolpo.*

BELOW LEFT *The gateway stupa to Ringmo, Dolpo.*

BOTTOM *The circular white patterns on the sides of adobe stupas in the Dolpo region are meant to help set off the medallion-like iconography. The winged figure seen here may be a Bön deity.*

OPPOSITE *Barren mountains dwarf a rustic stupa in Tarap, Dolpo.*

RIGHT *Stupas in Mustang's Lo region, a remote thumb of north-western Nepal enclosed on three sides by Tibet, are constructed almost entirely of mud bricks, clay, chalk and other earthen materials. Even the multitiered umbrella-spires on these stupas are made of brick.*

BELOW LEFT *Three* chortens *line a barren Lo Manthang ridge. The three monuments in the foreground are* lhato, *which commemorate the local earth spirits. The tricolour scheme pays homage to the Rigsum Gonpo, or three protector deities of Himalayan Buddhism: Chenrezig (Avalokiteshvara), Chenadorje (Vajrapani) and Jampeyang (Manjushri).*

BOTTOM *The Rigsum Gonpo colour scheme is divided among three separate* lhato *(shrines) at Tangbe, Lo.*

OPPOSITE *A roadside* lhato *in Lo displays the Rigsum Gonpo colouring as well as spherical decorations that mix Bön mandalas and Hindu-Buddhist icons.*

ABOVE *A typical Lo-style* chorten.

RIGHT *A brilliant collection of* chortens *and* lhatos *at Tangbe, Lo, creates a strong contrast with the lunar landscape, yet all the colourings come from local earth.*

BELOW *Two large Lo-style stupas at Tangbe stand next to two rows of four smaller stupas. The latter represent the eight classic Buddhist pilgrimage sites.*

OPPOSITE *This gateway stupa in Tsarang, Mustang, bears a strong resemblance to similar monuments in western Tibet.*

Another favoured style among the eight variations, especially in Tibet and Ladakh, is the 'turning of the wheel' model, which symbolises the Buddha's teachings and features square tiers cut with 'auspicious doorways' (typically, Buddha niches) along each side of the four-tiered base. A pane of glass or crystal may enclose the niches of more contemporary Himalayan stupas.

Tibet's five famous *kumbums* – monumental stupas found in Gyantse, Chung Riwoche, Jonang, Drampa Gyang and Dranang Jampaling – follow this model. Only Gyantse Kumbum escaped Chinese destruction. In the *kumbum* (literally, '100,000 Buddha images') the 'doorways' are expanded into substantial shrine rooms that may be filled with Buddhist sculpture and sumptuous mural paintings. Built in the mid-15th century, the incomparable Gyantse Kumbum is pocketed with 75 such shrine rooms, each containing interior murals of the classic Tibetan school, begun a century earlier in the Beijing workshops of the legendary Newari artist Aniko.

THE TIBETAN KUMBUMS

ABOVE *Along with Buddhist statuary, the shrine rooms at Gyantse Kumbum contain murals of the classic Tibetan school, which was developed by the artist Aniko.*

BELOW *The golden dome of Gyantse Kumbum rises like a crown above Pelkor Chode monastery, overlooked by the Gyantse Dzong (fortress), perched on a nearby crag.*

OPPOSITE *The kumbum at Dranang Jampaling was almost completely destroyed by the zealous Red Guard during China's Cultural Revolution.*

ABOVE *A demon figure at Gyantse Kumbum.*

ABOVE RIGHT *This photo of Dranang Jampaling, housed in the ruins of the monastery itself, shows what it looked like before the Chinese annexation of Tibet in the mid-1960s.*

FAR RIGHT *A statue of Yellow Tara, the Tantric goddess representing wealth and abundance, on the third floor of Gyantse Kumbum.*

BOTTOM *A statue of Amitabha, the Jina Buddha who presides over the 'Western Paradise' where his devotees will be reborn, stands in one of Gyantse Kumbum's shrine rooms.*

OPPOSITE *A Tibetan pilgrim performs a* kora *(circumambulation) of prostrations around Gyantse Kumbum.*

shrine rooms

bumpa

The Gyantse Kumbum contains
a total of 75 shrine rooms – there are
68 in the 20-cornered base levels;
four in the *bumpa*, or 'vase' dome;
and one each in the *harmika*, spire
and finial.

shrine rooms

bumpa

The Gyantse Kumbum contains
a total of 75 shrine rooms – there are
68 in the 20-cornered base levels;
four in the bumpa, or 'vase' dome;
and one each in the harmika, spire
and finial.

RIGHT *These whitewashed stupas, which appear to have thrust themselves out of the barren topography of Shey, in Ladakh, India, contain the remains of royalty and aristocrats from the 10th-century Shey Kingdom.*

BELOW LEFT *Children spin a row of prayer wheels attached to the base of a simple stupa.*

BOTTOM *The Potala, the palace-monastery of the Dalai Lama in Tibet, with Himalayan Buddhist stupas in the foreground.*

OPPOSITE *Tibetans spin prayer wheels near the Potala.*

Although it is often said that Himalayan stupas de-emphasise the stupa's original funerary character, many *gompa* (monastery) complexes of Tibet, Bhutan and other areas feature *chortens* that contain the remains of famous lamas or *tulkus*. At the Potala, the winter palace of the Dalai Lama since the 17th century, relics of several former Dalai Lamas are interred in *chortens*.

ABOVE *Hay is baled beside a series of crumbling stupas at Alchi Monastery in Ladakh, India.*

RIGHT *Himalayan stupas, their finials missing, line the road in Lamayuru, Ladakh.*

BELOW *The crenellated base of this stupa near the gompa in Shey suggests a variation on the 'auspicious doorways' archetype.*

OPPOSITE *At the Lamayuru Gompa stupas pierce the skyline like radio antennae in one of Ladakh's most spectacular settings.*

RIGHT *The dome niche on this reliquary stupa, at Drigung Til Monastery in Ü, Tibet, contains a small image of the lama whose relics are contained inside. The niche is rimmed with rare Tibetan beads, semiprecious stones and guardian deity reliefs.*

BELOW *At Tashilhunpo Monastery in Shigatse, an elaborate, gilded 11m stupa entombs the fourth Panchen Lama (1570–1662). Unlike many such funerary stupas, this one features steps ascending the tiered base, reminiscent of the 'descent from Tushita heaven' Himalayan stupa type.*

OPPOSITE *Studded with semiprecious stones, a stupa inside an assembly hall at Lhagang Monastery, Kham, contains the ashes of Yeshe Dorje, the 11th Karmapa (spiritual leader) in the Kagyüpa tradition.*

While stupa-building in all Buddhist traditions involves important religious preparations, such practices become especially important in Lamaism. Every stage of producing the Himalayan stupa is accompanied by copious ritual, including the recitation of specific mantras and the inscribing or attachment of *yantras* (sacred line drawings), mandalas or Buddhist canonical verse upon the various materials used. Long before even the first stone or brick is laid, the artisans and attending monks must follow prescribed ways of inspecting the proposed site, determining the cardinal directions, evaluating the soil, appeasing earth spirits and finally taking possession of the site.

The many ritualised contents of a Himalayan stupa vary according to local tradition and sponsorship, but among the mandatory constituents are *tsha-tsha*, hand-sized clay tablets impressed with images of Buddhist deities or stupas. In some cases the *tsha-tsha* may be moulded in the shape of simplified miniature stupas and filled with tiny prayer scrolls. As many as 100,000 *tsha-tsha* may be interred in a stupa. Most Himalayan stupa bases also contain five ceramic or metal vases (*kalasha* in Sanskrit, *bumba* in Tibetan), one for each cardinal point plus the centre, filled with a variety of sacred substances such as Tibetan herbs; precious metals; gems; mantra-inscribed strips of cloth; and *ringsel*, tiny, pearl-like crystalline balls said to be self-generated relics from the cremations of Buddhas or high lamas. Other items passed on from monastery to monastery over the decades – such as a piece from a highly revered monk's robe or walking staff – may also be enshrined to add to the stupa's *dharmakaya*.

The *tsok-shing* (axis pole running from the dome through the finial), another Himalayan stupa element treated with great respect, must be carved from sacred juniper, cedar or sandal and then wrapped in consecrated cloth, copper tubing, prayer inscriptions and other religious symbols. In some traditions, the *tsok-shing* may be embedded with relics and herbs. In many ways this central *axis mundi* represents the essence of the stupa, reaching back to the origins of the term in its association with a pole around which crops are heaped.

ABOVE *Inside Lhasa's Jokhang, Tibet's most sacred temple, a heavily ornamented stupa with an enlarged and bejewelled niche frame holds the remains of one of the temple founders.*

RIGHT *Three stupas in an assembly hall at Drepung Monastery, west of Lhasa, contain the relics of high lamas. In the 17th century, at the height of Drepung's influence, the monastery housed 10,000 lamas and monks, and served as the headquarters for the second, third and fourth Dalai Lamas.*

BELOW *On at altar at Katsel Monastery in Ü, a small gold reliquary stupa is squeezed between two Buddhist deity figures.*

OPPOSITE *Sera Monastery, founded in 1419 just north of Lhasa, is one of the most important centres for Tibet's Gelugpa order. A* chorten *containing the relics of a monastery founder is flanked by a photo and a painting of the 14th Dalai Lama, Tenzin Gyatso.*

Once a stupa has been built, ritual responsibility shifts from the monks, architects and sponsors to the visiting pilgrims. Although in all Buddhist lands, walking clockwise around stupas is considered an important way to earn religious merit, in the Himalayas the *kora*, or circumambulation, takes on even greater significance. While walking around the stupa in *kora* a devout Himalayan pilgrim will leave offerings of flowers at various cardinal points, perform prostrations, and utter prayers or mantras. According to the Tibetan sutras, as quoted by Chatral Sang-Gye Dorje Rinpoche:

Whoever pays reverence and respect to a stupa will become a non-returner [to the painful world of samsara] and will eventually completely and perfectly awaken to unsurpassed and utterly perfect enlightenment. Even if one offers only one prostration or makes one single circumambulation, one will be completely freed from going to places like the Avici hell. One will never fall away from unexcelled and completely perfect enlightenment.

FAR EAST VARIATIONS

OPPOSITE *Combining Indian and Central Asian influences, this unique stupa at Tayuan Si, one of many temple complexes at Wutai Shan, is thought to have been constructed around the same time that the great teacher Amoghavajra taught Tantric Buddhism there in the 8th century.*

By the beginning of the first millennium AD, Chinese traders had extended their caravan routes across the vast territories now ruled by China, across Central Asia and as far west as Asia Minor. Known today as the Silk Road, this network of foot, horse and camel tracks became a conduit for all manner of goods moving in both directions. Alongside the selling and bartering of silk, spices and tea, a steady trade in religious and philosophical ideas evolved. Among the most attractive to the Chinese – accustomed as they were to the non-theistic tenets of Taoism, perhaps – was Buddhism.

By the 4th and 5th centuries AD Chinese scholars began braving the Gobi Desert, high mountain passes and many other physical obstacles to visit the philosophy's source, India. One such pilgrim, Faxian (Fa-hsien), collected Sanskrit Buddhist literature, along with Buddhist devotional art, and after his return to China via Sri Lanka and Java 15 years later, he spent the remainder of his life translating these scriptures into Chinese.

Faxian also managed to compose the earliest known written chronicles of many of the areas in which he travelled. Although Faxian reported on Buddhist stupas encountered at Gandhara, Taxila, Purushapura (Peshawar) and Sri Lanka, the earliest known stupa in China is a square monument in Shandong with door niches on each side, topped by a tiered roof and short finial. Inscriptions date the monument to the last years of the Six Dynasties period, roughly a hundred years after Faxian's return.

The next renowned Chinese pilgrim to make the arduous journey to southern Asia, Xuan Zang (Hsuan Tsang, 602–64), spent 17 years travelling through 16 countries before returning to Chang'an, China, to write *Record of the Western Regions*. His imperial Tang dynasty sponsors were said to have been so impressed that they ordered the construction of the Dayan Ta (Big Goose Pagoda) in Chang'an in 648 to archive the Buddhist texts he collected.

Xuan Zang's contribution to Chinese Buddhism cannot be underestimated, and during the Tang dynasty (618–907) under which he lived, Buddhist arts flourished in China. Many brick stupas – called *ta* in Mandarin Chinese, or less commonly *cheti* – were constructed during this period, most of them modelled after the scant stupa architecture of the earlier Six Dynasties period.

Buddhist teachings and art flowed in the other direction as well, as monks from India found their way into the heart of China. One such teacher was Amoghavajra, a native of Samarkand (in present-day Uzbekistan) who studied Tantric Buddhism with Vajrabodhi in Java shortly before Borobudur was constructed. Teacher and student travelled to China together in 720, and although Amoghavajra went back to Java for a short time, Buddhists in China begged him to return.

During his long Chinese sojourn, the learned monk taught at a monastery on holy Wutai Shan (Five-Peak Mountain) in north-central China. A brick stupa from this era – or possibly earlier – still stands at the centre of this monastery. Although it follows the classic Indian design of base, dome and spire, the dome's slightly inverted curve brings to mind the Himalayan stupa, while the ringed finial has widened almost to form a tower.

LEFT *A stone relief of a winged ram at Wutai Shan.*

BELOW LEFT *At the complex of Wutai Shan, a statue of Guanyin (the Bodhisattva of mercy) sits atop a lion, her hands filled with cash offerings from Chinese devotees.*

BELOW RIGHT *A Mahayana Buddhist monk sounds a huge bronze temple bell at Wutai Shan.*

OPPOSITE *The 11th-century Baisikou tower stupas in Yinchuan, Ningxia, are of unequal height, most likely because they were built at different times by sponsors of differing means.*

Amoghavajra died in China 28 years later, leaving behind a stream of Tantric Buddhism called Chen-yen (True Word) that put mantras, *mudras* and Bodhisattva-filled mandalas at the forefront of Buddhist practice. The Bodhisattva Manjushri developed into such a central figure at Wutai Shan monasteries that even in remote areas of the Himalayas today Tantric Buddhists believe that Manjushri resides on the mountain. Presently over 40 Chinese Buddhist monasteries and 10 Tibetan lamaseries can be found among the mountain's five peaks.

Towards the end of the Tang era, Buddhism suffered through a period of persecution – perhaps in reaction to an increase in lavish, tax-exempt temple complexes – that resulted in the destruction of a great many works of Buddhist architecture at Chang'an and Luoyang.

During the ensuing Song dynasty (960–1279), most schools of Buddhism in China fused with Taoist and Confucian thought, and Taoist/Confucian shrine pavilions (sweeping tile roofs open at the front and supported by thick wooden pillars) began merging with the stupa styles from the 'western kingdoms'. Despite this shift in orientation, brick and stone remained the *ta* building materials of choice throughout the Song era. The use of such building components meant that sloping sides were usually necessary, thus preserving something of the overall tapering, dome-like nature of the Indian stupa.

Chinese twists on the formula, borrowed from the Taoist-Confucian shrine model, included heavy ridges or cornices to create separate levels along the full height of the monument, save for the finial. In this way the base and the dome became one, emphasising verticality and creating what stupa historian Adrian Snodgrass calls the 'tower stupa' or what many English speakers know today as the 'pagoda'.

One of the most famous Song-era tower stupas still standing is the Tie Ta (Iron Pagoda), so called because its structure of glazed brick makes it look – from a distance – as if it were made of iron. Built in 1049 in the city of Kaifeng, the tower's 13 storeys suggest the 13 ribs or rings of the Nepali or Tibetan stupa finial, while the octagonal plan recalls the Lanna or Lan Xang stupas of northern Thailand and Laos.

LEFT *Begun during the Tang dynasty (618–907), the Dali San Ta (Three Stupas of Dali) at Chongsheng Temple are major landmarks in northern Yunnan. The oldest and tallest of the three, 70m Qianxun Ta, features a square plan and 16 storeys, while the shorter, octagonal ones stand 42m and 10 storeys.*

BELOW *Kaifeng's Tie Ta, or 'Iron Pagoda', boasts 13 separate levels whose glazed-bricks, patterned in 28 different styles, give the monument a metallic appearance when viewed from afar.*

OPPOSITE *In what is perhaps the most common design among Chinese tower stupas constructed after the 10th century, a Song dynasty (AD 960–1279) tower at Liu Rong Temple, Guangzhou, displays an octagonal plan and 17 shrine levels. Atop the tower, a 5-tonne metal finial bears 1000 Buddhist sculptures.*

The Yingxian Mu Ta, the 'Wooden Pagoda' of Shanxi, took on further characteristics of the Taoist/Confucian/Buddhist pavilion, including the use of wood as a building material. Although wooden towers of this type didn't have the durability of brick or stone stupas, the medium opened the door to decorative innovations. Level cornices developed into roofs, and wood bracing at each level – often structurally redundant but allowing for more carving surfaces – bore elaborate patterns.

Interior spaces were lavishly appointed with mural paintings, deity altars and plenty of statuary. In this sense the Chinese tower stupas have much in common with the five great Tibetan *kumbums*, all of which were expanded examples of the classic 'stupa of auspicious doorways'. It has also been suggested that the Mahabodhi Stupa in Bodhgaya, India, may have influenced the development of the Chinese tower stupa, but this theory neglects the fact that many tower stupas in China are older than the Mahabodhi in its current form.

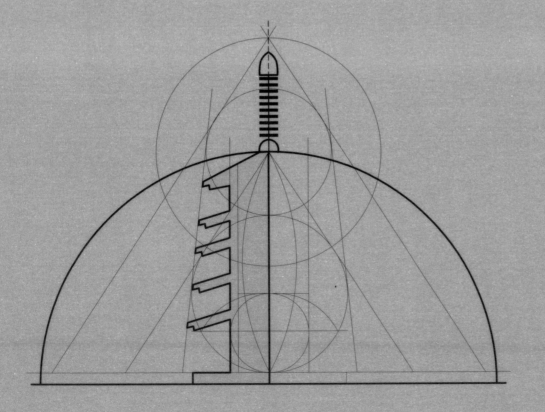

Some art historians postulate an 'invisible dome' for East Asian tower stupas.

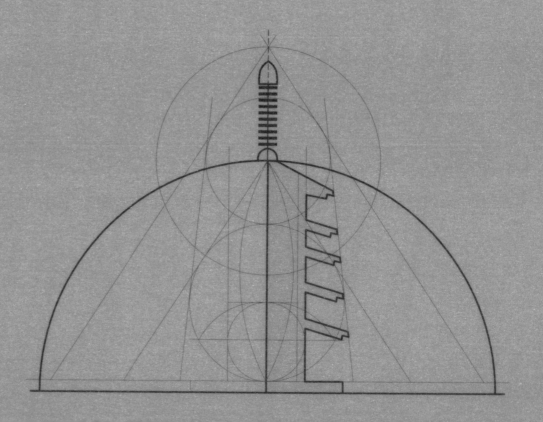

Some art historians postulate an

'invisible dome', for East Asian

tower stupas.

When Kublai Khan and his Mongol armies occupied much of China and installed their own Yuan dynasty (1279–1368), the country entered a period of religious tolerance previously unheard of. A Buddhist art renaissance followed in which the stupa briefly shed its Taoist/Confucian influence and returned to earlier forms. Because of historical connections, the Mongolian court was particularly supportive of Himalayan Lamaism, and we see in some of the religious monuments of this era touches of Tibetan inspiration.

One of the most distinctive Yuan-era stupas is the bottle-shaped Bai Ta in Beijing, which in its vaguely Himalayan style bears a striking resemblance to the famous stupa at Wutai Shan. Instead of a circular base and lotus-petal-adorned *harmika*, however, these features on Bai Ta exhibit the classic 20-cornered *vimshatikona* plan seen in many Nepali and Himalayan stupas.

LEFT *Tang dynasty rulers constructed Dayan Ta (Big Goose Pagoda) in Chang'an in AD 648 to archive Buddhist texts collected by renowned Chinese pilgrim Xuan Zang during his 17-year voyage through southern Asia. Here the verticality of Chinese stupas has become firmly established around a square plan with seven diminishing storeys.*

FAR LEFT *The oldest multistorey wooden structure in China, 67m Mu Ta in Ying County, Shanxi, is thought to have been erected in the 10th or 11th centuries. Such five-storey, octagonal designs served as partial models for Japanese tower stupas.*

BELOW *One of the most mysterious and undocumented stupa sites in China is this cluster of 108 stupas at Qingtongxia in northern China. Unlike the more common tower stupas found in China, the Qingtongxia monuments preserve the base-dome-spire designs typical of South and South-East Asia. It is believed that this site was constructed during the tolerant Yuan era (AD 1279–1368), when Himalayan Buddhist influences entered the Chinese religious milieu and influenced Buddhist architecture.*

OPPOSITE *Built during the Wan-li period of the Ming dynasty (1573–1619), the twin tower stupas of Yangzuo Monastery, Taiyuan exemplify the Sinitic preference for architectural symmetry. Made entirely of hand-shaped brick, each octagonal tower features 13 levels separated by vestigial roof lines whose cornices are carved to resemble wooden structures. Arched, niche-like windows in each side suggest the 'auspicious doorways' model of certain Tibetan stupas.*

It may have been that the isolated complex of 108 stupas – arranged in 12 rows of one to 19 stupas each, thus forming a huge triangle – at Qingtongxia near Yinchuan, northern China, was constructed during the Yuan era. Although there exists no epigraphic evidence dating the mystifying site, the individual stupas are almost identical in design to the Bai Ta in Beijing.

The Bai Ta, Wutai Shan and Qingtongxia stupas would have been stylistic exceptions, however, even under the Mongols, as 'tower stupas' continued to be the rule. Brick alternated with wood as a building material, but even when brick was used it was often carved to look like wood. The latter technique was used to great effect in the Ming dynasty (1573–1619) construction of Yangzuo Monastery's 'Twin Pagodas', where again we see 13 levels or storeys and an octagonal plan. The Chinese aesthetic preference for symmetry in fact led to a number of 'twin pagoda' monasteries where two identical tower stupas were raised.

Although Indian Mahayana Buddhism is the obvious wellspring, all schools of Buddhism in east Asia today have passed through Chinese filters that add a Sinitic twist to Indian or Tibetan forms of philosophy and worship. The naturalism of China's indigenous Taoism, for example, had a substantial influence on Chan Buddhism and its heirs in Korea (Son), Japan (Zen) and Vietnam (Thien). Avalokiteshvara, the Bodhisattva of compassion, became one of the most popular of all Buddhist deities among east Asians, and in the process switched genders from male to female (as Guanyin in China, Kannon in Korea and Japan, Quan The Am in Vietnam). The notion of 'emptiness', native to Taoism, took the early Mahayana concept of *shunyata* or 'the void' to new epistemological dimensions, reducing the concept from a metaphysical footnote to a central philosophy behind all schools of Sinitic Buddhism but one, Pure Land.

Pure Land (Qingtu) Buddhism, though it originated in China, flourishes today only outside that country. Chen-yen (True Word) Buddhism disappeared entirely in China but found a firm base in Japan as Shingon Buddhism after the legendary Japanese priest Kobo Daishi (774–835) studied under a Tantra master in China. That master, Hui Guo (746–805), had himself been trained by Buddhist teachers from Java, coincidentally making Java instrumental in the spread of Buddhism to Japan as well as to Tibet.

For the most part, the religious cultures of east Asia beyond China inherited the tower stupa wholesale, leaving behind any obvious connections with India or Tibet. One exception is Korea, where we do see large solid brick or stone structures (called *t'ap* in Korean) reminiscent of Tang era *ta* in China, particularly in Puyo and Kyongju. Most feature three, five or seven levels and were constructed under the Paekche and Shilla kingdoms, roughly mid-7th to mid-10th century. Later structures tended to be assembled of wood, as in China.

LEFT *An 8th-century Japanese monk built this* to *at Tanzan-jinja to commemorate the spirit of his statesman father, Fujiwara Kamatari. The roof lines of the tower's 13 storeys are so exaggerated as to almost completely obscure the shrine rooms.*

BELOW LEFT *Standing over 12m high, this gilded Kannon (Bodhisattva of mercy, equivalent to China's Guanyin) inside the 17th-century* hon-do *(main hall) at Hasedera Temple is the largest wooden image in Japan. Note the* kalasha *(auspicious vase) in its left hand.*

BELOW RIGHT *A stone* to *rises from among the trees in the garden of Shoren-in, a temple of the Tendai sect in Kyoto.*

OPPOSITE *During the last two weeks of November, the 17th-century* to *at Kiyomizu-dera in Kyoto is illuminated to showcase the surrounding autumnal foliage.*

As early as AD 530, Korean Buddhist monks, accompanied by architects and painters, sailed to the islands of Japan to teach Buddhism and temple construction. Strong links between the dynastic representatives of the two countries furthered the exchange of ideas, and Buddhism in Japan was largely codified under the reign of Prince Shotoku (574–622), who studied with Korean priests and then combined Buddhism with Confucianism, a religious fusion partially responsible for the creation of Japanese nationhood. The prince also established relations with China's Sui dynasty (589–618), thus opening the door to direct Chinese influence in all spheres.

Yet more Korean influence accrued to Japan when the Japanese colonised Korea from 1910 to 1945. Many Korean religious art treasures were taken to Japan during the colonial period, including the stone Pongsina Stupa, originally erected at Pudoam Monastery in 1620 during Korea's Choson era (1392–1910). Dismantled and shipped to Japan, the stupa ended up in the garden of the Osaka Municipal Museum until its return to Korea in 1987.

As in China and Korea, the tower stupa (called *to* in Japanese) is the norm in Japan today. The Japanese usually make a distinction between the tower stupa, equated with Shumisan (Mt Meru in Hindu-Buddhist cosmology) and smaller stone structures called *gorinto*, or less frequently, *sotoba*.

Gorinto literally means 'five (go) element (rin) pagoda (to)', a reference to its assembly of five stones. These stones are carved into shapes that represent the five elements – earth (cube), water (sphere), fire (triangle/cone), air (hemisphere) and space (gem/oval). Each level in a Shingon gorinto will be carved with one of the Sanskrit characters standing for the five seed mantras of Shingon – a, va, ra, ha and kha – which are associated with the five Jina Buddhas of Vajrayana Buddhism. A sixth Sanskrit syllable spread across the reverse side of all five stones is vam and represents the element of illuminated consciousness as well as Dainichi Nyorai (Mahavairochana in Sanskrit), confirming Shingon as a unique variant of Bengali Tantric Buddhism that developed en route to Japanese shores via Java and China.

BELOW LEFT *Mt Koya (Koya-san), the birthplace of Shingon Buddhism (perhaps the school closest to the original, esoteric Tantric Buddhism of Bengal) is home to more than 2000 temples, shrines, towers and stupas. This* gorinto *is almost completely buried in small stone votive stupas left by devotees.*

BOTTOM *In these classic Shingon gorintos at Mt Koya the assembly of five carved stones can clearly be seen.*

OPPOSITE *Originally built in the 8th century by Chinese residents, then rebuilt in 1426, the five-storey* to *at Kofuku-ji in Nara, Japan, features more extreme roof lines than its Chinese prototypes. This difference eventually became the norm for tower stupas throughout Japan. At nearly 50m, this is the second-highest tower stupa in Japan.*

Spatially the first three elements of the *gorinto* – cube, sphere and cone – correspond with the base, dome and spire of the traditional stupa, while the crowning hemisphere supporting an oval gem shape is reminiscent of the moon-and-sun finial of the Himalayan stupa. The relatively larger conical stone, however, so dominates the whole that it gives the impression of a roofline, thus connecting the overall aesthetic with that of the east Asian tower stupa.

In this fundamental change, as the stupa moved from west to east, one can see a diminishing or even erasure of the dome in favour of extending the base (bottom up) or extending the finial (top down). A metaphysical explanation might be that the dome has been rendered invisible and that, in the tower stupa, Mt Meru – the stupa's original and perhaps most basic representation – persists. One might also speculate that the axis pole aspect of the original stupa was being emphasised, inside the same imagined dome.

Throughout its long history, the stupa sustained its prototypical characteristics while undergoing gradual structural, architectural and artistic transformations as Buddhism travelled from one region to the next. Alternating preservation with adaptation, fidelity with innovation, each culture that accepted Buddhism developed its own models according to local artistic sentiments and, in many cases, local belief systems. However one chooses to explain the evolution of the stupa, the most salient feature shared by both Indic and Sinitic versions remains the same: encasement of the dharma.

GLOSSARY

Adi
'Primordial Buddha'; the original self-generated Buddha of Tantric Buddhism

Amoghavajra
teacher who studied in Java and travelled to China in 8th century AD; originator of Chen-yen (True Word) Buddhism

anda
literally 'egg'; the dome section of a stupa

Angkor
temple complexes (and their style of architecture) in north-west Cambodia, dating from 9th to 13th centuries AD

Ashoka
great Buddhist king of India, 3rd century BC

Atisha
Indian teacher who reformed Buddhist practice in Tibet in the 11th century AD

Avalokiteshvara
Bodhisattva of the current era, associated with compassion

bhikkhu
Buddhist monk

bhumi
the 13 'spheres' or stages in the ascent to nirvana

bhumisparsa
one of the *mudras*, or symbolic hand gestures, by which the Buddha calls the Earth to witness his enlightenment

bodhichitra
'awakened mind' or spiritual enlightenment

bodhi-ghara
carved rail enclosure for a Bodhi tree

Bodhi tree
the fig tree under which the Buddha was sitting when he attained enlightenment

Bodhisattva
one who has almost reached *nirvana*, but who renounces it in order to help others attain it; literally 'one whose essence is perfected wisdom'

Bön
pre-Buddhist religion of Tibet

Buddha
'Awakened One'; there are many Buddhas, but the term usually refers to the originator of Buddhism, born Siddhartha Gautama in India in the 6th century BC

buddhadharma
the teachings of the Buddha; the principles of Buddhism

butkadah
Persian idol temple

chaitya
Sanskrit word for stupa

chandi
Javanese stupa or shrine

chattravali
stylised umbrella or parasol, an ancient Indic symbol used to denote persons of royal rank or high spiritual status; the structure at the top of a stupa

Chen-yen
Chinese name for the 'True Word' sect of Buddhism

chita
Vedic funeral pyre

chiti
Vedic fire altar

chorten
Tibetan stupa

Confucianism
the ethical system of Chinese philosopher Confucius

dadar
Tibetan arrow symbol used in rites of fertility and longevity

dagaba
Sri Lankan stupa

Dalai Lama
one of 14 (so far) manifestations of *Avalokiteshvara* who, as spiritual heads of the Gelugpa order, ruled over Tibet from 1642 until 1959. The present 14th Dalai Lama resides in India

dashabala
the 10 powers of the buddhahood

devaraja
Hindu god-king

dharma
Buddhist moral code of behaviour; natural law

dharmachakra
'wheel of dharma'; wheel-shaped symbols representing Buddhist doctrine

dharmaduta
'dharma ambassadors'; Buddhist missionaries

dharmakaya
the 'body of the doctrine'

dharmaraja
king who rules in accordance with Buddhist dharma

dhatu
element; property

dorje
Tibetan word for the 'thunderbolt' symbol of Buddhist power; also a Tantric hand-held sceptre

dukkha
suffering; pain; distress; discontent

Faxian
Chinese translator of Buddhist literature and composer of the earliest known chronicles of South-East Asia

gala
'neck'; a common name for *harmika* in Kathmandu

gau
amulet containing sacred objects with powers of protection in the Himalayas

Gautama
(Pali: Gotama) family name of Siddhartha, the historical Buddha of the current age (6th century BC)

Gelugpa
'Yellow Hat Sect'; an order of Tibetan Buddhism founded by the monk Tsongkhapa in the 14th century; headed by the Dalai Lama

gompa
Tibetan monastery complex

gorinto
Japanese stupa assembled of five stones, representing the five elements and five seed syllables for Shingon Buddhist mantras

griha-stupa
literally 'house-stupa'; an Indian cave temple

Gupta
Indian dynasty, 3rd to 5th centuries AD

hamsa
the brahminy duck, a mythological bird sacred to Hindu-Buddhist traditions.

harmika
part of a stupa's superstructure: box-like unit on top of the dome

hti
Burmese word for the umbrella-like structure on top of a stupa

jatakas
tales of the previous lives of Buddha

Jina Buddhas
'Victorious Buddhas'; symbolic rather than historical, representing cosmic principles of the buddhadharma

Kagyüpa
an order of Tibetan Buddhism

kalasha
auspicious vases symbolising prosperity, placed in the foundation of stupas and sometimes carved into stupa reliefs

Kali Yuga
the present age, a dark age that has been in existence for approximately 5000 years

Karmapa
a lineage of spiritual leaders of the Kagyüpa order; also known as the Black Hats, there have been 17 so far

Kashyapa Buddha
the third Buddha of the current era

kora
Tibetan term for circumambulation, or walking around a stupa, to earn religious merit

Kubera
Hindu/Buddhist god of wealth

kumbha
'vase'; Tibetan stupa dome, which is wider at the top than the bottom

kumbum
literally '100,000 Buddha images'; monumental Tibetan stupa containing shrine rooms filled with statuary and paintings

Lamaism
a variety of Buddhism, chiefly followed in Tibet, so-called from the lamas (priests) belonging to it

lhato
a Himalayan shrine to local earth deities

mahachaitya
'great stupa', eg, the Great Stupa at Sanchi, in central India

Mahavamsa
'The Great Lineage'; early chronicle of Sri Lanka

Mahayana
'Great Vehicle'; a type of Buddhism which holds that the combined belief of its followers will eventually be great enough to encompass all of humanity and bear it to salvation; prevalent through East Asia, Tibet and Nepal

Maitreya
a Buddha who will come in a future era

mandala
'circle' in Sanskrit; geometrical symbol in Hindu and Buddhist art symbolising the universe, used as a meditation device; often the basis for the plan of a stupa

Manjushri
one of the two great Bodhisattvas of Mahayana Buddhism, who personifies wisdom

mantra
sacred word or syllable used by Buddhists and Hindus to aid meditation or invoke certain deities

Mara
the personification of evil and temptation

meuang
Thai word for city-states

Mt Meru
mythical mountain at the centre of the universe in Hindu-Buddhist cosmology, also known as Sumeru; it is this mountain that stupas are said to represent

mudras
symbolic hand gestures adopted by the Buddha

nagas
serpent gods

Newari Buddhism
a variety of Buddhism practised in the Kathmandu Valley, with close ties to Hinduism

Newars
people of the Kathmandu Valley

nirvana
the ultimate aim of Buddhist practice; final release from the cycle of existence

pahto
Burmese stupa with hollow interior

Pala
dynasty ruling Bengal, 8th to 12th centuries AD, known for its distinctive school of Buddhist art

pañchavasa
'five dwelling' monastery plan

parinirvana
the after-death state of nirvana

paya-dagagyi / paya-dagamagyi
'honoured stupa-builder' (male and female form); Burmese title given to one who has performed the meritorious act of building a stupa

peseva
Sinhalese word for passageways for stupa circumambulation

plii
'banana flower'; short, spire-like feature of stupas of Ayuthaya (Thailand)

pradakshina
circumambulation of a stupa for religious merit

Prajñas
female consorts for the five Jina Buddhas

prang
blunt-topped spire, common among stupas of Cambodia, patterned on Indian *shikharas* or temple spires

prasada
cube-like lower structure of Indian temples

prashavya
reverse (anticlockwise) circumambulation of a stupa

prathama deshana
the first teachings of the Buddha

puja
religious ritual with a specific purpose

Pure Land (Qingtu) Buddhism
form of Mahayana Buddhism devoted to Amitabha Buddha, who presides over the pure realm of the 'Western Paradise', where his devotees will be reborn

rab gnas
Tibetan term for the final ceremony in the consecration of a stupa

raja
Indian king

reuan thâat
semi-open relic chambers in stupas of Ayuthaya (Thailand)

Rigveda
the original and longest of the four main *Vedas*, or holy Sanskrit texts

ringsel
tiny crystalline balls said to be self-generated relics from the cremations of Buddhas or high lamas

rinpoche
literally 'high in esteem'; a title bestowed on highly revered lamas

sa blang
Tibetan earth-taking ritual in the consecration of a stupa

sabha
assembly hall in a monastery

Sailendra
Javanese dynasty, 7th to 9th centuries AD

samsara
the continuous cycle of death and rebirth

Sangha
the monastic community, forming the third aspect of the Buddhist 'Triple Gem', consisting of Buddha, Dharma and Sangha

Satya Yuga
'The Age of Truth'; the golden age

shikhara
tall corncob-like spire on an Indian-style temple

Shingon Buddhism
Japanese name for the 'True Word' sect of Buddhism

Shiva
the Hindu god of destruction and renewal

Shumisan
Japanese name for Mt Meru

shunyata
early Mahayana concept of 'the void'

sotoba
old Japanese word for 'stupa'

stamba
Persian-style pillar monument

t'ap
Korean stupa

ta
Chinese stupa

tanha
grasping, craving, thirst, selfish desire

Tantric Buddhism
a form of Buddhism that emphasises occult practices

Taoism
ancient Chinese philosophy that emphasises harmony with nature

Tara
Tantric female deity

thâat
Thai/Lao word for stupa

Theravada
'teaching of the elders'; a type of Buddhism which holds that the path to nirvana is an individual pursuit, prevalent in Sri Lanka, Myanmar, Thailand, Laos and Cambodia

Thupavamsa
'Chronicle of the Stupas'; the most complete collection of Pali writings on stupa lore

to
Japanese tower stupa

torana
tiered stone gateways

tower stupa
tall stupa of east Asia, often referred to in English as a pagoda

Tripitaka
Theravada Buddhist scriptures, divided into three categories, hence the name 'Three Baskets'

tsha-tsha
small votive images made of clay, often in the shape of a stupa, and sometimes filled with Tibetan prayer scrolls

tsok-shing
'life-tree'; Tibetan word for the centre axis pole of a Himalayan stupa

tulku
Tibetan Buddhist reincarnation of a great lama

uposatha
a hall in a monastery used for ordination ceremonies

Vairochana
(also known as Mahavairochana) 'Illuminator' or the 'embodiment of perfection'; one of the five Jina Buddhas

vajra
Buddhist 'thunderbolt' symbol, representing the power of wisdom

vajracharya
Newari Buddhist lay priest

Vajrayana
'Diamond Vehicle'; a branch of Buddhism originally from Bengal and now popular in Himalayan lands and Mongolia

vatadage
roofed pavilion thought to have once enclosed certain Sinhalese stupas

vedika
stone balustrade around the circumambulatory pathway, common in early Indian stupas

vihara
Buddhist monastic residence

vimshatikona
the basic 20-cornered shape for many Tantric mandalas, also occasionally employed for stupa plans

Vipaswi Buddha
the first Buddha of the present era

yahsi
Nepali word for central axis pole of a stupa

yajña
Hindu fire sacrifice

yantra
geometric diagram thought to create energy

yoni
female fertility symbol linked with the Hindu cult of Shakti

zedi
Burmese stupa

Joe Cummings has contributed to more than 35 original guidebooks, phrasebooks, maps, atlases and photographic books for Lonely Planet and other publishers. He has served as a tourism industry consultant for Unesco and for PATA, and designed itineraries for Asia Transpacific Journeys and Geographic Expeditions. Joe lives across the road from an 18th-century Shan stupa in Thailand.

Bill Wassman has been photographing Asia and Europe since 1975 and has contributed images to dozens of publications around the world. He has been honoured with a Pacific Area Travel Association (PATA) Gold Award for his work in Nepal, and was one of 50 photographers chosen to cover Thailand for the Kodak-sponsored *Seven Days in the Kingdom*. Stupas have been a growing obsession ever since he first spotted Svayambhunath Mahachaitya in 1968. Bill divides his time between New York, Ibiza and Kathmandu.

ACKNOWLEDGMENTS

We would like to thank the following people for their invaluable help with research and logistics: Stan Armington, Keith Dowman, Bruce Evans, Charles Gay, Andreas Kretschmar, Arthur Mandelbaum, Kerry Moran, Tom Pritzker, Alexander Rospatt, Pam Ross, Thomas Schrom and the Patan Museum, Heidi Spielhagen and Ted Worcester. Special thanks to Tej Hazarika of Cool Grove Press for early concept development and to Professor Robert AF Thurman for writing the foreword.

PHOTO CREDITS

Bill Wassman
all photographs, except the following:

Joe Cummings
p42; p84 bottom left; p96 bottom left;
p96 bottom right; p99; p114 2nd from left

Alexander Rospatt
p114 3rd from left; p115 3rd from right
and far right; p116 far left

Charles Gay
p115 2nd from right; p116 2nd from left

Nabaraj Sanjel
p116 3rd from left

Luca Tettoni
p49

Sara-Jane Cleland
p26 bottom centre

Bernard Napthine
p60 bottom left; p66 bottom left

Juliet Coombe
p72 bottom

Bradley Mayhew
p142 bottom

Di Mayfield
p160 left

ILLUSTRATIONS

INDEX